SIXTY GLORIOUS YEARS

OUR QUEEN

Elizabeth II

DIAMOND JUBILEE

1952 – 2012

First published in 2012

A catalogue record for this book is available from the British Library

ISBN: 978-0-857331-65-6

Published by Haynes Publishing, Sparkford, Yeovil,
Somerset BA22 7JJ, UK
Tel: 01963 442030 Fax: 01963 440001
Int. tel: +44 1963 442030 Int. fax: +44 1963 440001
E-mail: sales@haynes.co.uk
Website: www.haynes.co.uk

Haynes North America Inc., 861 Lawrence Drive,
Newbury Park, California 91320, USA

Images © Mirrorpix

Creative Director: Kevin Gardner
Designed for Haynes by BrainWave

Printed and bound in the US

SIXTY GLORIOUS YEARS

OUR QUEEN

Elizabeth II

DIAMOND JUBILEE

1952 – 2012

VICTORIA MURPHY

CONTENTS

INTRODUCTION

Since Queen Elizabeth II succeeded to the throne 60 years ago Britain has seen huge social, political and economic change.

In six decades the country and its people have gone through 12 Prime Ministers, four recessions, wars and a technological revolution.

No one has observed these changes more acutely than the Queen herself, as she travels the length and breadth of the country, visiting thousands of families in their homes, on the streets and in their meeting places.

Ten years ago, at her Golden Jubilee celebrations, she observed: "For if a Jubilee becomes a moment to define an age, then for me we must speak of change – its breadth and accelerating pace over these years."

Yet, decade after decade, the Queen has remained a constant – a stable figure in an ever-shifting world.

"I declare before you all that my whole life whether it be long or short shall be devoted to your service and the service of our great imperial family to which we all belong."

Princess Elizabeth on her 21st birthday, 21st April 1947

Through rain or shine, conflict or peace, and in times of great joy or great sorrow, her determination to carry out her duties and connect with her people has not faltered.

Before she even became queen, at the tender age of 21, Princess Elizabeth pledged: "I declare before you all that my whole life whether it be long or short shall be devoted to your service and the service of our great imperial family to which we all belong."

When she made the declaration more than 60 years ago it was a promise yet to be fulfilled.

Today, as she approaches 60 years on the throne, those words can be looked back on as a motto of her long and glorious reign – her vow has been made good 10, 20, 60 times over.

Many people watched television for the first time ever in 1953 when the grainy pictures of the 27-year-old queen's Coronation were broadcast.

By the time she celebrated her Silver Jubilee in 1977 colour images of the celebration were beamed into virtually every home in the land.

And when she marks 60 years on the throne in 2012, the spectacle will be shared on thousands of laptops, iPads and mobile phones, with the royal Twitter, Facebook and YouTube sites leading the way.

No one can know what advances the next decade will bring, but we can be sure that, through her determination to keep the Royal Family relevant to its people, the Queen will embrace them.

Turning 86 in her Diamond Jubilee year, the Queen is a mother, grandmother and now great-grandmother, and her family continues to grow and adapt to its ever-changing demands on the world stage.

Sixty Glorious Years celebrates her extraordinary ability to secure a place in the hearts of generations as Britain moves further into the 21st Century.

CHAPTER ONE

PRINCESS ELIZABETH
1926 – 1951

"Daughter born to the Duchess of York."

The *Daily Mirror* headline, Thursday 22nd April 1926

RIGHT: **Princess Elizabeth aged six months, October 1926.**

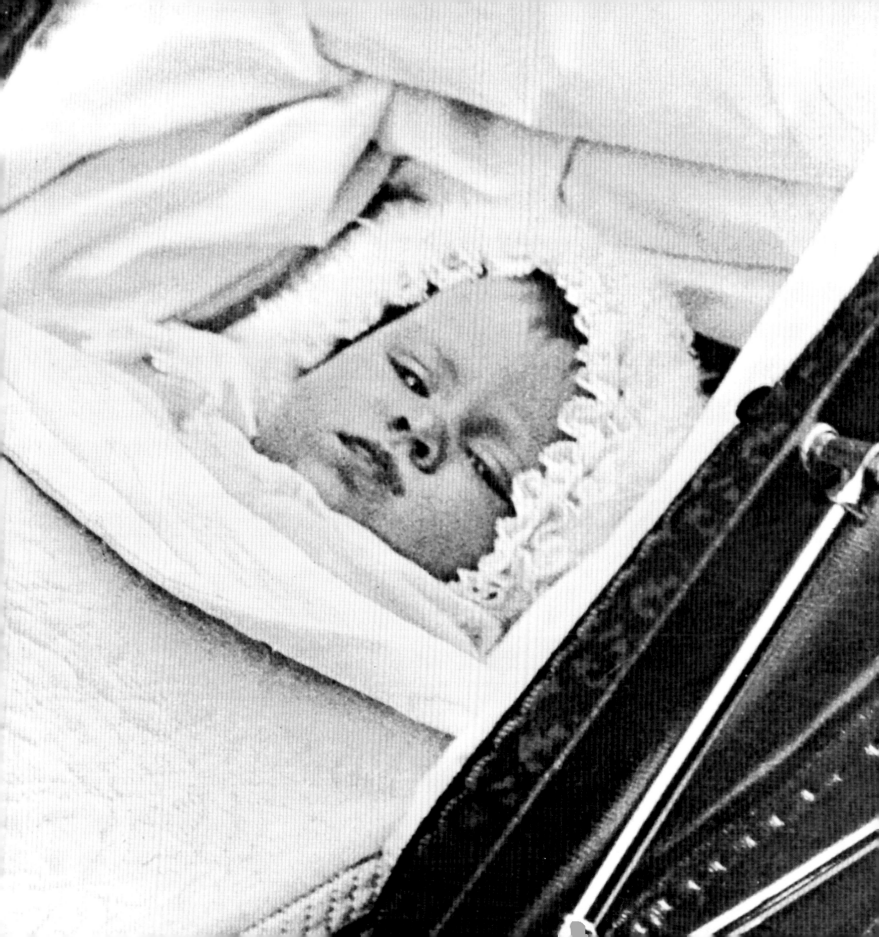

EARLY LIFE

When Princess Elizabeth Alexandra Mary came into the world at 2.40am on 21st April 1926 it was never expected she would one day be queen. As granddaughter of the reigning monarch, George V, she was technically third in line to the throne, but no one believed her father would ever become king, let alone that she would succeed him just a few years later.

It was her uncle, Edward, Prince of Wales, who was due to inherit the crown, while Elizabeth's family was very much the side-show.

Her parents, Prince Albert and Lady Elizabeth Bowes-Lyon, who had become the Duke and Duchess of York when they married on 26th April 1923, brought up Elizabeth and her little sister Margaret away from the limelight. Theirs was an idyllic childhood, with time divided between their impressive London town house at 145 Piccadilly, the palatial White Lodge in Richmond Park, and later the Royal Lodge in Windsor Great Park where the family moved when Elizabeth was six.

Described as "jolly" and "well-behaved", she was affectionately known as "Lilibet" to her family, a name those closest to her still use today. The two sisters were educated at home by their governess, Marion Crawford, nicknamed Crawfie, who was later ostracized by the palace for writing a tell-all book about her time there called *The Little Princesses*. Crawford tried to make sure the privileged sisters were given an introduction to life outside royal circles, with trips to the zoo and travels on the London underground. Elizabeth's passion for horses and dogs and her dutiful and thoughtful personality shone through from an early age. "She has an air of authority and reflectiveness astonishing in an infant", Winston Churchill said about her when she was only two, and her diligence in her studies saw her become fluent in French, a skilful horse rider and a strong swimmer.

ABOVE: **Princess Elizabeth aged two with her parents, the Duke and Duchess of York, 1928.**

RIGHT: **The York family in the 1930s. Elizabeth's only sibling, Princess Margaret Rose, was born on 21st August 1930.**

ABOVE: **King George V and Queen Mary in 1911, a year after he became king.**

RIGHT: **Princess Elizabeth with her grandparents, King George V and Queen Mary, on the way back to Balmoral after attending church at nearby Crathie, 5th September 1932.**

LEFT: Princess Elizabeth and Margaret arrive with their mother for the 1933 Royal Tournament at Olympia. The tournament was an annual military tattoo and pageant which ended in 1999.

BELOW: Princess Elizabeth aged nine at the sixth birthday party of the Master of Carnegie at Elsick House, Aberdeenshire, with Margaret and friends, 23rd September 1935.

THE KING'S DAUGHTER

The York's peaceful existence was shattered in 1936 when King George V died.

Elizabeth's uncle, her father's older brother, came to the throne as Edward VIII. But he abdicated only 11 months later under a cloud of controversy to marry the woman he loved, the twice-divorced American socialite Wallis Simpson. As Edward was exiled to France, Elizabeth's father, a shy awkward man with a stammer, became king – taking the name George VI.

Elizabeth's destiny was thus sealed. It was a moment that was not lost on her high-spirited little sister Margaret who reportedly said: "Does that mean you're going to be queen? Poor you."

Life as the princesses knew it changed overnight as the family moved into Buckingham Palace with its 775 rooms and army of servants. Thrust into the limelight and faced with the challenge of restoring public confidence in the monarchy, King George VI worked hard to make sure his eldest daughter was prepared for the moment she would inherit responsibility for the crown.

But the next few years were not easy for the family since, along with the rest of the country, their world was turned upside down by the Second World War. While their parents stayed in Buckingham Palace to show solidarity with their people, Elizabeth and Margaret spent most of the war at Windsor Castle, sheltering in the dungeons as the German planes roared overhead.

It was during this time, on 13th October 1940, that Elizabeth made her first public broadcast on BBC *Children's Hour*. In a clear, high-pitched voice, the 14-year-old princess declared "all will be well" and told Britain's evacuated children: "My sister Margaret Rose and I feel so much for you as we know from experience what it means to be away from those we love most of all."

It was the first of many speeches Elizabeth would make in her lifetime to the people of Britain in moments of joy and sadness, and her flawless, heartfelt delivery gave a first glimpse of the accomplished leader she was to become.

Two years later she carried out her first solo public engagement, spending a day with the Grenadier Guards, the beginnings of a life spent meeting her people and sharing their stories. And when Britain celebrated the end of the war, taking to the streets and waving flags, Elizabeth and Margaret left the sanctuary of Buckingham Palace to parade through London with the throngs below.

RIGHT: **King George VI, his wife Queen Elizabeth, his mother Queen Mary, Princess Elizabeth and Princess Margaret on the balcony of Buckingham Palace after his Coronation, 12th May 1937.**

SATURDAY, MAY 15, 1937

Daily Mirror

No. 10436　　　Registered at the G.P.O. as a Newspaper.　　ONE PENNY

KING GEORGE VI AND HIS QUEEN
ROYAL CORONATION PORTRAIT

Their Majesties King George VI and Queen Elizabeth, with their daughters, the Princess Elizabeth and Princess Margaret Rose—a Coronation portrait specially taken at Buckingham Palace. A Coronation portrait of the Royal Family is on pages 14 and 15, with pictures of the presentation of Coronation medals to members of the Overseas contingents by the King and Queen. Further pictures of this ceremony are on pages 5, 12 and 17.

ABOVE: Guests gather inside Westminster Abbey for the Coronation of King George VI and Queen Elizabeth, 12th May 1937.

LEFT: *Daily Mirror* front page, showing King George VI's Coronation portrait, 15th May 1937.

ABOVE: **Former King Edward VIII, here the Duke of Windsor, pictured with wife, Wallis Simpson, in their Paris home after his abdication; date unknown.**

ABOVE LEFT: Princess Elizabeth aged 12 in the royal box at Aldershot Tattoo, 1ˢᵗ June 1938.

ABOVE RIGHT: Princess Elizabeth aged 12, smiling as she steps out of a car, March 1939.

ABOVE: Princesses Elizabeth and Margaret buy war savings certificates at a post office, 1943.

RIGHT: King George VI and his family inspect crops at Sandringham during the Second World War. They are using a pony trap and bicycles to save petrol, 13th August 1943.

LEFT: Princess Elizabeth learning car maintenance after she joined the army as a mechanic, 12th April 1945.

ABOVE: **Prime Minister Winston Churchill joins the Royal Family on the balcony of Buckingham Palace on Victory in Europe Day to celebrate the end of the Second World War, 8ᵗʰ May 1945. After this picture was taken Elizabeth and Margaret went, unnoticed, outside the palace walls to join the crowds.**

LEFT: **Princesses Elizabeth and Margaret and their mother at a garden party in Durban South Africa, 1940s.**

BELOW: **Princess Elizabeth being initiated into the Bardic circle at the Welsh National Eisteddfod, Mountain Ash, Glamorgan, August 1946.**

RIGHT: **Princess Elizabeth launches HMS *Eagle* in Belfast, 19th March 1946.**

ABOVE LEFT: **Princess Elizabeth dancing with Captain Lord Rupert Nevill at the Royal Merchant Navy Ball in London's Dorchester Hotel, 5ᵗʰ May 1946.**

ABOVE RIGHT: **Princess Margaret with Group Captain Peter Townsend. They were photographed together in Kimberley during the Royal Family's four-month tour of South Africa in 1947. Townsend was equerry to the King from 1944, and he and Margaret fell in love and wanted to marry. But this was not permissible because he was divorced, and their ill-fated romance caused the royals much controversy in later years.**

RIGHT: **King George VI presents an award to the Paramount Chief on a visit to Bechuanaland during the Royal Family's four-month tour of South Africa in 1947. It was on this tour that Princess Elizabeth turned 21 and made one of her most moving speeches, pledging to devote her life to her country.**

MARRIAGE

No one knew it at the time, but even in the earliest years of her work, the princess had already met the man who was to be by her side through the many royal duties to come.

Elizabeth first set eyes on Prince Philip of Greece and Denmark at a wedding in 1934. Their paths crossed again in 1939 at the Britannia Royal Naval College, Dartmouth, when she was 13, and from then on she was smitten. Worried she was too young to marry, her parents tried to quell her passion and encouraged her to focus her mind on royal duties. But after years of exchanging letters and enjoying all too brief meetings, it became clear that Elizabeth's desire was not going to fade, and King George VI eventually agreed to let his daughter marry the man she loved.

Philip may not have been the perfect choice of husband, being virtually penniless and with a family tree that brought him a little too close for comfort to Nazi Germany. But he had served for Britain in the war, and his good looks, blue blood and obvious devotion to Elizabeth won the day.

They were married on 20th November 1947 at Westminster Abbey and thousands lined the streets to see the princess, who had already stolen the nation's hearts, pledge her love for her prince. The princess wore an ivory satin dress, which was bought with ration coupons, and the couple received more than 2,500 presents and 10,000 telegrams of love and support. Philip, who had already adopted the British name Mountbatten from his paternal grandparents before the engagement announcement, was given the title Duke of Edinburgh on his marriage.

The *Daily Mirror* called it "a day of smiles" and mentioned that King George VI had raised his glass and said: "Our daughter is marrying the man she loves."

After the thrill of the celebrations, the couple retreated to Broadlands in Hampshire, followed by a trip to Birkhall on the Balmoral Estate, for a honeymoon before settling into married life.

Soon they had their own little family, with the birth of Prince Charles on 14th November 1948, followed by Princess Anne on 15th August 1950. Shortly after his son came into the world, Philip's naval career took him to Malta, and Elizabeth divided her time between his base and their London home of Clarence House. She relished the weeks spent with her handsome husband on the Mediterranean island. Under the radar, and with Charles looked after by nannies, she was able to enjoy the quiet freedom of any naval wife, the weight of her future role momentarily lifted from her young shoulders.

But these carefree moments did not last for long. With her father's health deteriorating, Elizabeth began to take on more royal duties, and the prospect of her inheriting the crown became increasingly real. When the King had to pull out of a tour to Australia and New Zealand because of his worsening lung cancer, Elizabeth and Philip boarded the plane on 31st January 1952 to take his place. Inside the privacy of the aircraft as the 3,000-strong crowd waited outside, the 25-year-old princess said goodbye to her father. It was the last time she saw him.

RIGHT: Princess Elizabeth and new husband Philip Mountbatten gaze lovingly at each other on their wedding day, 20th November 1947.

ABOVE: Philip Mountbatten on his stag night, the day before marrying Princess Elizabeth, 19th November 1947.

RIGHT: Princess Elizabeth arrives at Westminster Abbey with her father for her wedding on 20th November 1947. Her dress was designed by Norman Hartnell, had a 13-foot train and was embroidered with thousands of pearls and white beads.

The King later wrote his daughter a touching letter, telling her: "I was so proud of you & thrilled at having you so close to me on our long walk in Westminster Abbey, but when I handed your hand to the Archbishop I felt that I had lost something very precious. You were so calm & composed during the Service and said your words with such conviction, that I knew everything was all right."

ABOVE: **The wedding party pose for a photograph in the Throne Room of Buckingham Palace after the marriage of Princess Elizabeth and Philip Mountbatten.**

LEFT: **Crowds line the streets of London to see the royal wedding procession, 20th November 1947.**

RIGHT: **Royal wedding cake, 20th November 1947.**

LEFT: **Princess Elizabeth and the Duke of Edinburgh on their honeymoon in Broadlands, Hampshire, 28th November 1947.**

RIGHT: **Princess Elizabeth and the Duke of Edinburgh in Paris, 11th May 1948.**

LEFT: **Princess Elizabeth with her first baby, Charles Philip Arthur George, second in line to the throne, at his christening on 15th December 1948. When he was born on 14th November 1948, crowds cheered outside Buckingham Palace as the BBC Home Service announced "The princess and her son are both doing well" before playing the national anthem.**

BELOW: **Princess Elizabeth dancing an Eightsome Reel at the Saddle Club dance, Malta; date unknown.**

LEFT: **Princess Elizabeth and her husband with Prince Charles and Princess Anne, 1951.**

RIGHT: **The Queen and Philip took a coast-to-coast tour of Canada in 1951. It was their first visit there and they travelled 10,000 miles round the country by land, sea and air.**

CHAPTER TWO

A NEW QUEEN
1952 – 1954

"I am sure that this, my Coronation, is not the symbol of a power and a splendour that are gone but a declaration of our hopes for the future, and for the years I may, by God's Grace and Mercy, be given to reign and serve you as your queen."

Queen Elizabeth, Coronation speech, 2nd June 1953

RIGHT: Queen Elizabeth II and the Duke of Edinburgh, with their children on the balcony at Buckingham Palace on Coronation Day, 2nd June 1953.

ACCESSION

When Princess Elizabeth became queen she was thousands of miles from home, asleep in the Treetops Hotel in the wilds of Kenya.

The exact moment of her accession to the throne is not known, but King George VI died in the night between 5th and 6th February 1952 at Sandringham, after suffering a fatal blood clot in his heart. He was aged 56 and in the 16th year of his reign, and although he had been plagued with lung cancer for some time, his death shocked the nation.

Flags in every town flew at half-mast, all sports events and TV programmes were cancelled, Parliament was suspended and all cinemas and theatres were closed. Prime Minister Winston Churchill said: "We cannot at this moment do more than record the spontaneous expression of grief." The tragic news took several hours to reach the remote part of Kenya where Elizabeth was staying, and it was her husband Philip who eventually told his 25-year-old wife she was now queen.

In a BBC radio broadcast that day, reporter Frank Gillard said: "How tragic to think that even this morning as she sat at breakfast talking about her father and proudly describing how bravely he had stood up to his illness and how well he had recovered, sitting there in her yellow bush shirt and brown slacks, even at that moment her father was lying dead, and she had succeeded to his vast responsibilities." He added that when, at about 2.45pm local time, Elizabeth was told of her father's death, "in the words of a member of a household she bore it like a queen".

Two hours later Elizabeth left the lodge, giving a sad little wave to small crowds outside. She had left Britain just six days earlier a young princess and mother, and now she was returning to begin a new life as the country's sovereign, a huge responsibility on such young shoulders.

Two days after her father's death, on 8th February 1952, Elizabeth read her Accession Declaration in front of 150 privy counsellors in St James's Palace. She said: "By the sudden death of my dear father I am called to assume the duties and responsibilities of sovereignty… My heart is too full for me to say more to you today than I shall always work, as my father did throughout his reign, to advance the happiness and prosperity of my peoples, spread as they are all the world over." Proclamations of her accession were then made all round the UK.

That year the new queen made her first Christmas Day broadcast from Sandringham, and said: "Since my accession ten months ago, your loyalty and affection have been an immense support and encouragement."

RIGHT: Princess Elizabeth and Philip at Treetops in Kenya on 5th February 1952, the day before her father, King George VI, died in his sleep and she succeeded him as queen.

ABOVE: The new Queen Elizabeth arrives home in Britain on 7th February 1952, after returning from Kenya following the death of her father, King George VI. She is met by a solemn line of British dignitaries including Prime Minister Winston Churchill.

LEFT: Crowds gather at the gates of Buckingham Palace following the announcement of the death of King George VI, 6th February 1952.

ABOVE: Crowds gather in London to hear the reading of the Proclamation of Queen Elizabeth II, 8th February 1952.

RIGHT: King George VI's body lies in state at London's Westminster Hall for three days before his funeral from 12th to 15th February 1952.

KING GEORGE VI FUNERAL

LEFT: Funeral procession of King George VI. The procession passed through the streets of London from 9.30am as the first of Big Ben's 56 chimes began – one for every year of his life. The King's body lay in state in Westminster Hall for three days before the funeral, when more than 300,000 people visited to pay their respects. He was buried at St George's Chapel, Windsor Castle, 15th February 1952.

BELOW: Three queens in mourning. Queen Elizabeth, her mother Queen Elizabeth, and her grandmother Queen Mary at the funeral of King George VI, 15th February 1952. George VI was the third son Queen Mary had seen die, and she passed away just one year later on 24th March 1953, aged 85.

ABOVE: **Queen Elizabeth, husband Philip and sister Princess Margaret at the Badminton Horse Trials, less than a month before her Coronation, 12th May 1953.**

LEFT: **The Queen shakes hands with Blackpool footballer Stanley Matthews as his team are presented the FA Cup trophy following their victory over Bolton Wanderers in the 1953 FA Cup Final at Wembley Stadium, 3rd May 1953.**

CORONATION

Virtually the whole of Britain came to a standstill to celebrate the Coronation of Queen Elizabeth II.

After months of intense preparations, the ceremony took place in Westminster Abbey on 2nd June 1953, by which time Elizabeth had been on the throne for more than a year.

Homes and streets round the country were scrubbed clean and festooned with decorations and flags in honour of the celebration, and despite the pouring rain, an estimated 3 million people lined London's roads, many camping out all night to get a good spot from which to watch the lavish military spectacle as it paraded past.

In an unprecedented move, after a long battle between the media and palace officials, cameras were set up inside Westminster Abbey and more than 20 million people worldwide saw the broadcast, which was translated into 44 languages. Many Brits watched TV for the first time in their lives that day, piling into friends' houses to catch a glimpse of the grainy black-and-white picture of the long, elaborate ceremony.

Elizabeth arrived at the Great West Door of the Abbey at precisely 11am to make her slow procession up the central aisle past the 8,000 invited guests. Her long, thick robes were so heavy that she found it hard to drag them behind her on the carpet and had to ask Dr Geoffrey Fisher, the Archbishop of Canterbury, to "Get me started."

In the Coronation Oath Elizabeth swore to govern her countries according to their laws and customs, to uphold the law and justice with mercy, and to protect the Church of England. Then, seated on the Coronation Chair, she was handed the four symbols of authority – the orb, the sceptre, the rod of mercy and the royal ring of sapphire and rubies. When the Archbishop of Canterbury placed the heavy St Edward's crown on her head, a shout of "God Save the Queen" was heard and a 21-gun salute was fired from the Tower of London.

As the Coronation procession made its way home to Buckingham Palace, crowds pressed up against the railings shouting "We want the Queen, we want the Queen."

At the tender age of 27 Elizabeth II had been officially crowned, and she took her new responsibility, and the Coronation's symbolic union between her and her people, very seriously. In a radio broadcast she said: "I have in sincerity pledged myself to your service, as so many of you are pledged to mine.

"Throughout all my life and with all my heart I shall strive to be worthy of your trust."

The Queen and Philip made a final appearance on the Buckingham Palace balcony at midnight, as fireworks lit up the London skyline, bringing the memorable Coronation Day to a spectacular close.

RIGHT: **Queen Elizabeth leaves Westminster Abbey after her Coronation, 2nd June 1953.**

ABOVE: Residents of Pine Street, Newcastle, decorate their street in preparation for a Coronation street party, 2nd June 1953.

LEFT: Crowds gather at London's Trafalgar Square to watch the Coronation procession with periscopes, 2nd June 1953.

RIGHT: A Manchester street decked out with decorations ahead of the Coronation of Queen Elizabeth II, 18th May 1953.

ABOVE: The Duke of Edinburgh kneels in homage to his wife after she has been crowned queen, 2nd June 1953.

LEFT: A bored-looking Prince Charles, aged just four, sitting between the Queen Mother and Princess Margaret in the royal box in Westminster Abbey, Coronation Day, 2nd June 1953. During the ceremony reporters spotted Princess Margaret casually brushing a piece of fluff from the uniform of Group Captain Peter Townsend. It was from this moment that the country realized they were in love and a nationwide debate began about whether they should be allowed to marry, a fact unthinkable at the time because he was divorced.

RIGHT: The Queen's official Coronation portrait, 1953. Her dress was designed by Norman Hartnell, whose sketches were unveiled the day before the event. The white satin gown was embroidered with gold and silver thread and pastel silks and encrusted with seed pearls and crystals. The design incorporated the floral emblems of the Commonwealth countries at the time: the Tudor rose of England, thistle of Scotland, Welsh leek, Irish shamrock, the wattle of Australia, maple leaf of Canada, New Zealand fern, South African protea, lotus flowers for India and Ceylon, and Pakistan's wheat, cotton and jute.

ABOVE: The Royal Family appear before the crowds on the Buckingham Palace balcony after the Coronation ceremony, 2nd June 1953.

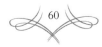

LEFT: *Daily Mirror* souvenir edition, celebrating the Coronation, 3rd June 1953.

BELOW: Queen Elizabeth and the Royal Family on her Coronation Day, 2nd June 1953.

COMMONWEALTH TOUR

Five months after she was crowned, Elizabeth and her husband embarked on a six-month tour of the Commonwealth. Leaving Charles and Anne at home with their nannies, the couple waved goodbye on 24th November for the epic voyage that would see them travel 43,618 miles by land, sea and air. They stopped in Bermuda, Jamaica, Fiji and Tonga, then New Zealand and Australia, before going onto the Coco Islands, Ceylon, Aden, Uganda, Malta and Gibraltar.

The couple were given rapturous applause wherever they went by fascinated crowds who could not get enough of Britain's glamorous new young sovereign.

The Queen's 1953 Christmas Day broadcast was made from New Zealand and she told the nation: "Of course we all want our children at Christmas time – for that is the season above all others when each family gathers at its own hearth.

"I hope that perhaps mine are listening to me now and I am sure that when the time comes they, too, will be great travellers."

The couple sailed home on the new Royal Yacht Britannia, a vessel the Queen was to become very attached to throughout her reign, arriving back in London on 15th May to cheering crowds and a 41-gun salute.

ABOVE: **The Queen and Philip on the bridge of the liner *Gothic* as it arrives at the Miraflores Locks in the Panama Canal during the royal tour. The Queen often has her camera with her to take her own photographs of her trips, 30th November 1953.**

LEFT: **Just a few days after she was crowned, on 11th June 1953, Elizabeth attended her first Trooping the Colour as queen, a military spectacle held annually on the sovereign's official birthday in June. Elizabeth rides her favourite horse, Winston, side-saddle.**

ABOVE: The Queen in Fiji with the governor, Sir Ronald Garvey, 29th December 1953.

LEFT: The Queen inspects a Naval guard of honour at Auckland, New Zealand, December 1953.

ABOVE: **The Queen and Philip drive through crowds of schoolchildren during a visit to Sabina Park, Kingston, Jamaica, November 1953.**

LEFT: **The Queen and Philip with the crew of HMAS *Australia* during their visit to Cairns.**

ABOVE: **The Queen makes her Christmas Day broadcast from Government House, Auckland, New Zealand, 25th December 1953.**

RIGHT: **The Queen climbs over rocks to see a cave in Waitomo, New Zealand, during the Commonwealth tour, 11th January 1954.**

OPPOSITE: **The Queen dresses in her finery for the Civic Ball in Hobart City Hall on a visit to Tasmania during the Commonwealth tour, 1st March 1954.**

CHAPTER THREE

SETTLING IN
1955 – 1965

"Though you have conquered Earth and chartered Sea
And planned the courses of all Stars that be
Adventure on, more wonders are in Thee."

Extract from "The Wanderer" by John Masefield, Poet Laureate 1930 to 1967.
The Queen read this extract during her Christmas Day broadcast in 1955.

RIGHT: Queen Elizabeth II and Philip the Duke of Edinburgh at Royal Ascot, 20th June 1956.

TEETHING PROBLEMS

Queen Elizabeth had enjoyed a spectacular start to her reign, with a Coronation that uplifted Britain, and a Commonwealth tour that went down a storm worldwide. But her new role was a hugely challenging one, and during the next few years she found herself negotiating some tough personal and professional problems.

The first had been looming for a while: Princess Margaret's relationship with divorced Group Captain Peter Townsend. From the moment the press noticed Margaret flick fluff from Townsend's uniform at the Coronation, the nation had been captivated by their love affair. But with the Church of England, of which the Queen is head, strongly opposed to divorce, and Parliament refusing to consent to their wedding, their love was doomed. As soon as the establishment found out about the relationship Townsend was posted overseas to Brussels, and a national debate raged about whether he and Princess Margaret should be allowed to marry.

The Queen tried to help them, at first telling the couple to wait a year, but it eventually became clear that Margaret had to choose: Renounce all her royal rights and privileges or give up her love. On 31st October 1955 Margaret issued a statement saying: "I would like it to be known that I have decided to not marry Captain Peter Townsend." It was over.

Their separation was a painful time for the Queen, who knew exactly what it was like to be young and in love. Despite her position she was powerless to help her sister. But Elizabeth also had the nation's problems to think about, and in 1956 the country was plunged into the Suez Crisis.

The troubles began in July when the Egyptian president, Colonel Gamal Abdel Nasser, nationalized the Suez Canal, the main supply of oil for Britain and France. That October,

British, French and Israeli troops sprang into action and began bombing Egypt to regain control of the canal. But their use of military force was condemned by the rest of the world and, humiliatingly, Prime Minister Anthony Eden was forced to call a ceasefire. It was a humbling and stressful time for Britain.

Not long after, Anthony Eden resigned because of ill health and Harold Macmillan took over as prime minister. In her Christmas speech that year the Queen spoke of the "family of nations" and said: "None the less, deep and acute differences, involving both intellect and emotion, are bound to arise between members of a family and also between friend and friend, and there is neither virtue nor value in pretending they do not."

That Christmas was also the first Elizabeth had spent without her husband Philip, who had gone off alone on a Commonwealth tour on the Royal Yacht Britannia. His lone voyage sparked rumours of marriage problems, and it wasn't long before the American press reported they were having a "rift". They speculated that Philip was fed up playing second fiddle to his wife and was frustrated at his lack of official role. The rumours persisted so much that the palace issued an unprecedented denial, with the Queen's press secretary, Commander Richard Colville, saying: "It is quite untrue that there is any rift between the Queen and Duke of Edinburgh."

The couple were reunited in February 1957 and, in a sign of her admiration for him, the Queen promoted her husband – giving him the official title of Prince Philip. They were soon travelling the world together again – visiting Canada and America in October 1957 where the Queen was hailed as the "Belle of New York".

LEFT: Prime Minister Winston Churchill escorts the Queen to her car after his resignation dinner at 10 Downing Street, 5th April 1955. Elizabeth was called upon to use her royal prerogative for the first time to appoint his successor, Anthony Eden.

BELOW: Peter Townsend leaving the Queen Mother's home of Clarence House, 14th October 1955. This was at a time when the country was waiting to find out if he would be allowed to marry Princess Margaret.

LEFT: The Queen, Queen Mother, Prince Charles and Princess Anne at a polo match in Windsor Great Park, 6th June 1955.

BELOW: The Queen stamping down the earth during a break in a polo tournament at Windsor Great Park, 14th June 1955.

LEFT: Crowds watch the Queen and Philip say goodbye to King Adeniji-Adele II on the outskirts of Lagos. The royal couple were enjoying a three-week royal visit to Nigeria, which lasted from 28th January to 16th February 1956.

BELOW: Queen Elizabeth and Philip meet the Emir of Kano during their visit to Nigeria, February 1956.

RIGHT: The Queen meets Marilyn Monroe, with Victor Mature on her right and Anthony Quayle on her left, at the Royal Film Performance of *Battle of The River Plate*, 29th October 1956.

ABOVE: **Philip on his lone tour of the Commonwealth on the Royal Yacht Britannia. He is with his friend, Mike Parker, 5th February 1957.**

LEFT: **The Queen and Philip reunited in Portugal after a separation of four months, 18th February 1957. He wears a tie with hearts on.**

ABOVE: **Prince Charles at his school sports day, watched by the Queen and Princess Anne, 9th July 1957.**

LEFT: **The Queen and husband Philip arriving at Albert Pier in Jersey on a visit to the Channel Islands, 30th July 1957.**

RIGHT: **The Queen and Philip wave to the Danish royal family, 26th May 1957.**

ABOVE: The Queen meets Bruce Forsyth and Eartha Kitt at the Royal Variety Show, 3rd November 1958.

TOP: **The Queen congratulates Judy Garland on her Royal Variety performance, 18th November 1957.**

ABOVE: **The Queen meets Frank Sinatra at the London premiere of *Me and the Colonel*, 27th October 1958.**

RIGHT: **The Queen arrives at the installation of the Order of the Thistle in Edinburgh, 4th July 1958.**

EXPANDING AND EXPLORING

Through her determination to master her role and resolve to put her country first, the young Queen was quickly winning both the love and respect of her public. And Elizabeth didn't just attend glamorous events and accept bows and curtseys – she showed she was keen to get stuck in and experience the life of the country's workers.

Royal visits became less formal, and the Queen happily donned white miners' overalls and a hard hat at Rothes Colliery in June 1958 for a 40-minute tour 500 feet underground. The *Daily Mirror* wrote: "Hats off for the pithead Queen", reporting how her practical outfit was given "one touch of femininity – a white nylon scarf over her head, ears and neck which, besides keeping coal dust out kept her hair in place".

She tirelessly toured the country on engagement after engagement, visiting families in their workplaces, their meeting places, and even in their homes. And it wasn't long before her own family expanded. Rumours of a marriage rift were well and truly squashed when, in August 1959, it was announced the Queen was pregnant with her third child. Prince Andrew was born on 19th February 1960, and just a week later there was more good news for the family as it was announced Princess Margaret would marry flamboyant photographer Antony Armstrong-Jones.

The Queen was thrilled that her sister had finally put her heartbreak over Peter Townsend behind her, although, ironically, Margaret's marriage was to eventually end in divorce.

Britain was now heading into the Swinging Sixties, bringing about huge cultural and political changes.

The once majestic British Empire was now almost defunct, and between 1945 and 1965 the number of people under British rule outside the UK fell from 700 million to 5 million. But in its place the Commonwealth was booming, and as its head the Queen was celebrated the world over as she toured the globe. She became the first reigning monarch to visit India for 50 years in 1961.

And the Queen was a host as well as a guest. In June 1961 she entertained President John Kennedy and his wife Jackie at Buckingham Palace, where both women dazzled in sumptuous evening gowns. Just two years after that meeting, on 22nd November 1963, the President was assassinated by a gunman in Dallas, Texas. Like the rest of the world, Britain was in shock, and the Queen led her country's tributes to Kennedy in a Westminster Abbey memorial service.

Her family's personal life also attracted some attention that year when 14-year-old Prince Charles was caught sipping cherry brandy in a bar during a Gordonstoun school trip in June. "Charles will have to face the music", said the *Daily Mirror*.

However, just a few months later the focus shifted onto happier family affairs, when it was announced the Queen was expecting her fourth child. Prince Edward was born on 10th March 1964, and her family was complete.

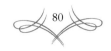

Her pregnancies with Andrew and Edward were the only times during her reign that the Queen did not perform the official State Opening of Parliament, a celebrated annual ritual. But pregnancy did not shield her from political controversy in October 1963 when she was called upon to use her royal prerogative to appoint a new prime minister after Harold Macmillan resigned. On Macmillan's advice she chose Lord Home, but the decision sparked a backlash and a bitterly fought leadership contest. Home lasted less than a year and the Conservative Party lost the next election, making Labour's Harold Wilson the Queen's fifth prime minister. In 1965 the Conservative Party brought in an elected procedure to choose their party leader, and the Queen has not played any part in their leadership changes since.

That year was also a sad year for the party and the Queen when her first prime minister and trusted friend, Sir Winston Churchill, died aged 90. As the man who led Britain through the Second World War, he was given an impressive state funeral where thousands turned out to pay their respects. But, as a sign that the country had moved on from the war, 20 years after VE Day the Queen and Philip made a historic 11-day visit to Germany, the first by a British monarch for 52 years. Their stop in West Berlin was a delicate tour in a city still bitterly divided by a cold stone wall, but they were greeted by cheers from almost a million people as they paraded through the streets.

In her Christmas speech that year the Queen told the nation: "In fact it is just because there are so many conflicts in the world today that we should reaffirm our hopes and beliefs in a more peaceful and a more friendly world in the future."

ABOVE: **The Queen in her mining outfit preparing to go down the mine at Rothes Colliery, 30th June 1958.**

LEFT: The Queen laughs as Officer B R J Hailstone issues the rum ration on board aircraft carrier HMS *Eagle* off the coast of Weymouth, Dorset, 29th April 1959.

BELOW: The Prime Minister of Ghana Dr Nkrumah at Balmoral Castle with the Queen, Prince Philip, Prince Charles and Princess Anne, 12th August 1959.

RIGHT: The Queen receives a flower from a little girl after unveiling a memorial to members of the Commonwealth Air Forces at Green Island, Ottawa, during a six-week tour of Canada and the US, July 1959.

ABOVE: **The Queen and Prince Philip with President and Mrs Eisenhower during their six-week tour of Canada and the US, 1st September 1959.**

BELOW: **Princess Margaret and fiancé Antony Armstrong-Jones read telegrams congratulating them on their engagement, 26th February 1960.**

LEFT: The happy couple wave from the Buckingham Palace balcony on their wedding day. Antony Armstrong-Jones was made Earl of Snowdon on their marriage, 6th May 1960.

ABOVE: The Queen and Prince Philip visit the council house of Mr and Mrs Llewellyn in Newton Aycliffe, where they ate home-made fruit cake, Durham, 27th May 1960.

LEFT: **The Queen Mother with her grandchildren Charles, Anne and Andrew, in the garden of Clarence House after they helped her open her 60th birthday presents, 4th August 1960.**

BELOW: **The Queen, Prince Philip, Charles, Anne and Andrew on Andrew's first holiday to Balmoral, 8th September 1960.**

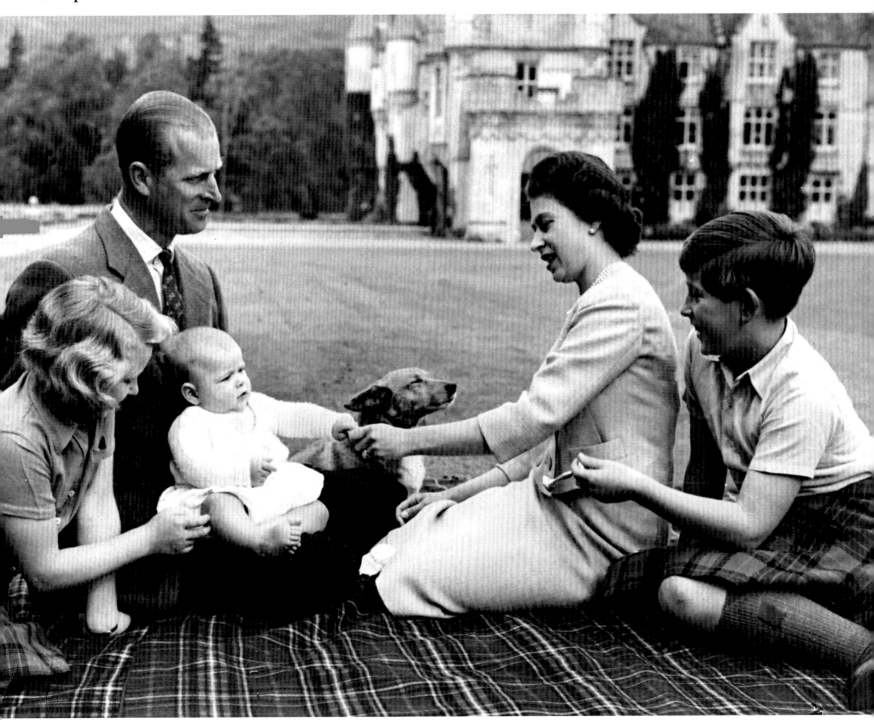

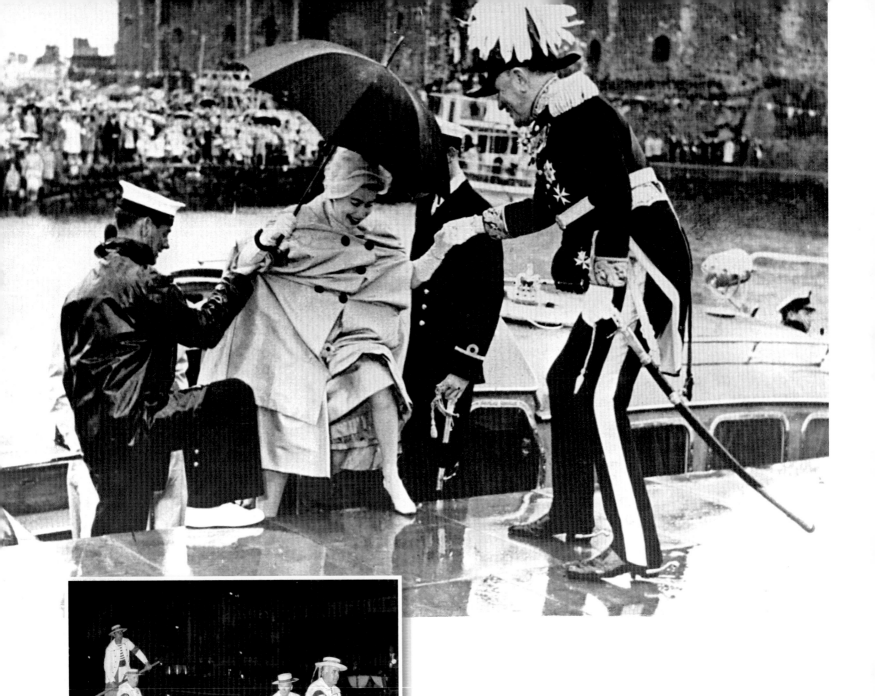

ABOVE: On 8th August 1961, crowds watched from afar as the Queen climbed ashore in Carrickfergus, Northern Ireland, for the start of her visit.

LEFT: The Queen and Prince Philip in Venice in a gondola, 8th May 1961.

RIGHT: The Queen receives a bouquet from little Mamawo Kaikai in the Kenema District of Sierra Leone, 30th November 1961.

ABOVE: The Queen and Prince Philip laugh together during a visit to Bathurst in Gambia, 5th December 1961.

RIGHT: The Queen at a Buckingham Palace garden party, summer 1962. Garden parties have been a royal tradition since the 1860s and every year the Queen hosts at least three at Buckingham Palace and one at Holyroodhouse – a total of more than 30,000 people attend. At a typical party 27,000 cups of tea are served along with 20,000 sandwiches and 20,000 slices of cake.

LEFT: The Queen and Prince Philip at Buckingham Palace together with President Kennedy and wife Jackie, 6th June 1961.

RIGHT: The Queen, Anne, Andrew and Edward in the grounds of Windsor Castle, summer 1964.

BELOW: Crowds clamour to look through the car windows as the Queen leaves Balmoral with baby Edward and Andrew, summer 1964.

LEFT: The Queen crosses the Forth Road Bridge with Prince Philip to open the bridge, 5th September 1964.

RIGHT: The Queen, Anne and Charles in the crowds at the Badminton Horse Trials, 11th April 1965.

BELOW: The Queen leads mourners at the state funeral of Winston Churchill, 30th January 1965. Prince Philip offers a final salute to the man who led Britain through the Second World War.

ABOVE: **A rare picture of the Queen driving herself, 1965.**

ABOVE: **The Queen accompanied by Willy Brandt, the West German Chancellor (on the Queen's left) and Prince Philip at the rear of the group, tour West Berlin, 27th May 1965.**

CHAPTER FOUR

MASTERING HER REALM

1966 – 1976

"Mankind has many blemishes, but deep down in every human soul there is a store of goodwill waiting to be called upon."

The Queen's Christmas broadcast, 1966

RIGHT: **The Queen meets actor Bill Travers and actress Virginia McKenna at the royal film show of** *Born Free*, **15th March 1966.**

JOY AND SORROW

The day England won the 1966 World Cup remains one of the greatest moments in the country's history, and the Queen was right at the heart of the celebrations.

When Bobby Moore's team beat West Germany 4-2 in the final on 30th July 1966 crowds at Wembley Stadium and all round the country went wild. The Queen and Philip were just two of the 93,000 faces in the stadium that day, and they were swept along in the euphoria as a smiling Elizabeth presented the captain with the trophy.

But, just three months after the joyful celebrations, the Queen joined her people in great sorrow as she toured the site of the Aberfan disaster.

It took only five minutes for the coal tip above the Welsh mining town to slide down the mountain on 21st October 1966, smothering 116 children and 28 adults. But the consequences would last a lifetime.

Queen Elizabeth faced some criticism for not visiting Aberfan immediately, but when she and Prince Philip did go there, on 29th October, she sobbed as she spoke with mothers who had lost their children. And, as she viewed the crushed homes, the Queen received a posy from a little girl with a card that read: "From the remaining children of Aberfan."

ABOVE: **The Queen meets the England football team at the opening ceremony of the 1966 World Cup at Wembley, 11th July 1966.**

ABOVE: The Queen and Prince Philip listen to the stories of the families in disaster-hit Aberfan, 29th October 1966.

ABOVE: The Queen presents Bobby Moore with the Jules Rimet trophy following England's World Cup win, 30th July 1966.

RIGHT: The House of Lords during the State Opening of Parliament, 22nd April 1966. The Queen conducts the ceremony every year.

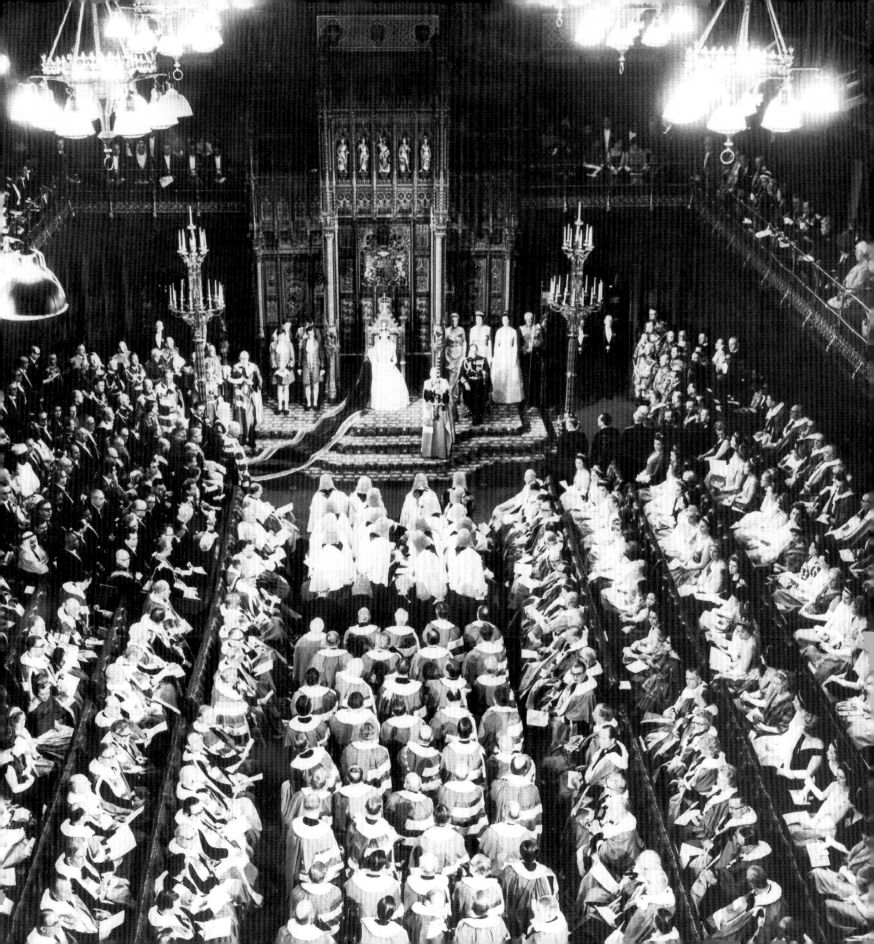

MILESTONES

In summer 1967 the Queen spent six days travelling through Canada to celebrate the country's Centennial – the 100th anniversary of the forming of the Canadian Confederation. On 1st July in Ottawa she made a speech in French and English and said: "It is altogether right and fitting that Sovereign and people should meet together here at the heart and centre of Canadian existence to give thanks on this great occasion."

Now in her 40s, the Queen was a confident and strong monarch, the eager girlishness of her early reign replaced by a more grounded maturity. And her own children were rapidly growing up, with heir Prince Charles celebrating his 21st birthday on 14th November 1969. In honour of his coming of age the Queen crowned him the Prince of Wales in a ceremony at medieval Caernarfon Castle in front of 4,000 guests on 1st July that year. She had given Charles the title when he was nine, but the ceremony signified the fact she thought he was mature enough to understand the responsibility.

In connection with his Investiture, which was televised, a special documentary film was also screened the night before, called *Royal Family*. The fly-on-the-wall film showed footage of the Queen, her husband and her children relaxing and going about their everyday lives in an unprecedented level of exposure. For the first time the public had behind-the-scenes access to Buckingham Palace. The film was wildly popular and about two thirds of British people tuned in to watch the first screening.

This was a new era of celebrating the normal and down-to-earth side of the Royal Family, in the hope of bringing them even closer to their people. The Queen's engagements had already lost some of the distant and formal nature of those of previous monarchs, and in 1970 this was taken one step further when she and Prince Philip created the "walkabout". The practice, now a staple part of all royal visits, started during their spring 1970 visit to Australia and New Zealand, when they began mingling with the crowds clamouring to see them.

The walkabout is now considered one of the most essential parts of royal engagements, but Princess Anne later admitted she hated the idea at first. In a 2002 interview she said: "A 19-year-old suddenly being dropped in the middle of the street and being told to go and pick on someone and talk to them. Fun? I don't think so."

As she grew up the Queen's only daughter became known for two things – her no-nonsense attitude and her formidable horse-riding skills. In 1971, the same year that she turned 21, Anne was crowned European Champion at three-day eventing and won the title BBC Sports Personality of the Year. And, unlike her older brother who waited until his 30s to settle down, Anne's engagement to Captain Mark Phillips was announced just two years later on 30th May 1973.

Crowds lined the streets, and 100 million people watched on television, as Anne made her way down the aisle of Westminster Abbey in her Tudor-style dress. And, in her Christmas broadcast that year, the Queen said: "I am sure that all parents seeing their children getting married are reminded of the continuity of human life."

ABOVE: The Queen and Prince Philip wave from the platform at the launch of the *QE2* at the John Brown Shipyard in Clydebank, Scotland, 20th September 1967. Her maiden voyage took place two years later on 2nd May 1969 from Southampton to New York City. Since then she has carried more than 2.5 million passengers before being decommissioned in 2008.

LEFT: **The Queen visits Prince Charles on his last day of school at Gordonstoun, 31st July 1967.**

ABOVE: The Royal Family on their horses at Royal Ascot races, 21st June 1968.

LEFT: Sean Connery meets the Queen at the premiere of *You Only Live Twice,* **12th June 1967.**

LEFT: The Queen and Prince Philip wave from their car during a visit to Salvador, Brazil, 6th November 1968.

BELOW: The Queen and Prince Philip with football legend Pelé at the Maracanã Stadium in Rio de Janeiro, 13th November 1968.

ABOVE: King Olav of Norway greets the Queen as she arrives in his country on 13th June 1969. Prince Andrew, Prince Edward and Princess Anne follow behind.

LEFT: The Queen and Princess Anne arrive back in London's Liverpool Street with their corgis after their Christmas break in Sandringham, 4th February 1969.

RIGHT: A scene from the BBC fly-on-the-wall documentary *Royal Family*. The Queen and Prince Philip work on their private jet, 1969.

ABOVE: **The Queen crowns Prince Charles as the Prince of Wales. He was given a sword, coronet, mantle, gold ring and gold rod during the religious ceremony in Welsh and English, 1st July 1969.**

RIGHT: **The Queen and Prince Charles leave Caernarfon Castle after the ceremony, 1st July 1969.**

LEFT: The Queen travels on the underground after opening the Victoria line, 7th March 1969.

RIGHT: The Queen, Prince Philip, Prince Charles and Princess Anne at a ceremony to dig the first piece of earth for a new cathedral at Frobisher Bay, Canada, 7th July 1970.

BELOW: The Queen, Prince Philip and Princess Anne at the British Embassy in Vienna during a state visit to Austria, 8th May 1969.

SILVER WEDDING ANNIVERSARY

"If I am asked today what I think about family life after 25 years of marriage, I can answer with equal simplicity and conviction. I am for it."

Queen Elizabeth, silver wedding anniversary speech at London's Guildhall, 20th November 1972

ABOVE: The Queen and Prince Philip on their silver wedding anniversary procession with Prince Charles, 20th November 1972.

RIGHT: The Royal Family official photograph for Elizabeth and Philip's silver wedding anniversary.

PRINCESS ANNE

ABOVE: **The Queen with Princess Anne, who was competing at three-day eventing for the first time, 26th April 1971.**

RIGHT: **Princess Anne arriving at the altar of Westminster Abbey on her wedding day to Captain Mark Phillips, 14th November 1973.**

ABOVE: **The couple leave the Abbey to cheering crowds, 14th November 1973.**

FAMILY TIES

The year before her only daughter married had been one of mixed emotions for the Queen. She had celebrated her silver wedding anniversary in November, riding through the streets of London to cheers and making a heartfelt speech at London's Guildhall. But the Royal Family also came together for a much sadder reason in 1972 – the death of the Duke of Windsor, once King Edward VIII.

In May that year the Queen had began a five-day visit to France, where she went to see her exiled uncle at his Paris home. He had been ill for some time and could not make it down to tea in the drawing room, but Elizabeth spent 15 minutes alone upstairs with him. Ten days later he died, and the Queen invited his once reviled American widow, Wallis Simpson, to Buckingham Palace for his funeral.

At the service in St George's Chapel, Windsor, attended by political leaders and diplomats, the Garter of Arms described him as "sometime the most high, most mighty and most excellent monarch Edward VIII".

Later, there was more sadness for the royals when Prince William, the Queen's cousin and then ninth in line to the throne, was killed in a plane crash, aged just 30. Thankfully, tragedy was narrowly avoided two years later, on 20th March 1974, when a kidnap attempt on Princess Anne was foiled. Anne was travelling along the Mall with husband Mark Phillips, just four months after their wedding, when their Rolls-Royce was forced to a halt by a Ford Escort. The driver of the Escort jumped out and fired at the royal party, injuring two police officers, Princess Anne's chauffeur and a nearby journalist. He then told Anne to get out of the car and come with him for a day or two because he wanted £2 million, to which Anne replied: "Not bloody likely." Thanks to the bravery of the police and onlookers, the kidnap plot was foiled and 26-year-old gunman Ian Ball was sent to prison indefinitely under the Mental Health Act.

Two years later there were more family worries for the Queen when Princess Margaret's separation from Lord Snowdon was announced. Buckingham Palace released a statement, and the couple appealed for understanding for their two children, 14-year-old Viscount David Linley and 11-year-old Sarah Armstrong-Jones. By this time it was well documented that they did not have a happy marriage, and that Margaret had sought comfort in the arms of younger lover, Roddy Llewellyn. Her divorce to Snowdon was finalized in May 1978. Ironically, the Queen's sister, who was unable to marry a divorced man, was now, 20 years later, the first member of the Royal Family to divorce since Henry VIII.

The Queen's 50th birthday on 21st April marked another milestone, which she celebrated with a family party at Windsor Castle. In July 1976 she and Philip visited America for the country's celebration of the 200th anniversary of the Declaration of Independence, and President Ford and his wife Betty held a White House dinner dance in their honour.

In her Christmas speech that year the Queen said: "Reconciliation, like the one that followed the American War of Independence, is the product of reason, tolerance and love, and I think Christmas is a good time to reflect on it."

RIGHT: The Queen, Prince Philip and Princess Anne at the Istana in Singapore, 20th February 1972.

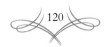

OPPOSITE: **The Queen chatting to housewives on a visit to Newcastle; date unknown.**

LEFT: **The Queen bends down to get a good look under the frame of one of the boats made by local fishermen of the Maldives Islands during a royal visit there, 14th March 1972.**

BELOW: **The Queen and Philip on a boat during a royal visit to Malaysia, 8th March 1972.**

LEFT: The exiled Duke of Windsor and his wife, Wallis Simpson, at their Paris home before his death; date unknown.

LEFT: **The Queen and Prince Philip with Wallis Simpson on the day of the Duke of Windsor's funeral in London, 5th June 1972.**

BELOW: **The Queen, with Prime Minister Edward Heath, attending a Fanfare for Europe, 3rd January 1973. This was a gala evening at the Royal Opera House, Covent Garden, to celebrate Britain's entry into the European Economic Community on 1st January 1973.**

Daily Mirror

EUROPE'S BIGGEST DAILY SALE

ANNE AND MARK IN GUN TERROR

Assassination bid: Royal detective hurt

THE SHOT BODYGUARD

LEFT: *Daily Mirror's* front page on Princess Anne's attempted kidnap, 21st March 1974.

BELOW: **Princess Anne at the hospital bedside of PC Michael Hills who was shot in the stomach during her attempted kidnap. He was awarded the George Medal for his bravery. Her protection officer, Inspector James Beaton, who was also shot, was awarded the George Cross, and pedestrian Ron Russell, who helped defend Anne, was awarded the George Medal. Journalist Brian McConnell, chauffeur Alex Callender and Detective Constable Peter Edmonds, who also helped Anne, were awarded the Queen's Gallantry Medal, 23rd May 1974.**

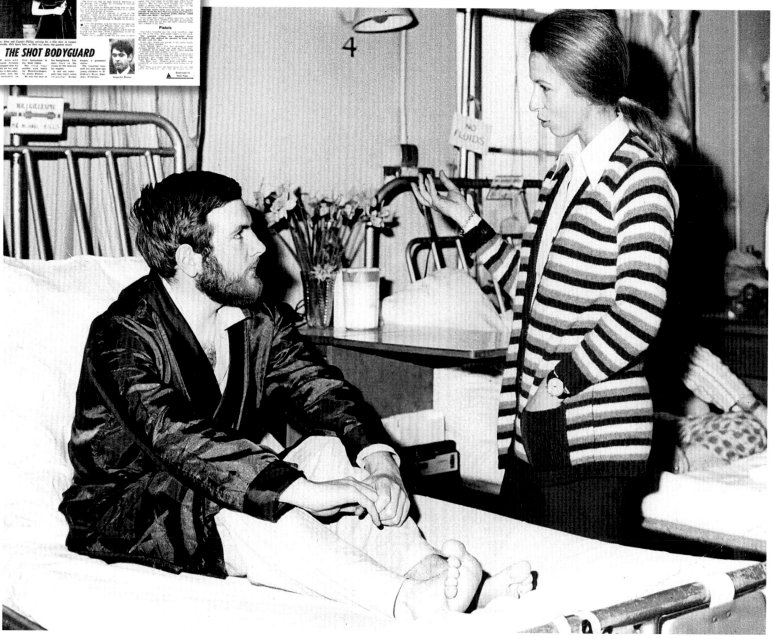

ABOVE: **The Queen at Trooping the Colour, 17th June 1974.**

ABOVE: **The Queen roars with laughter at a joke by the daughter of Detective Inspector James Beaton, who was awarded the George Cross for protecting Princess Anne, 27th November 1974.**

LEFT: **The Queen dances with President Ford during a state dinner in honour of her state visit to America, 7th July 1976.**

RIGHT: **The Queen visits the *Daily Mirror*, 26th February 1976.**

CHAPTER FIVE

SILVER JUBILEE
1977

*"When I was twenty-one I pledged my life to the service of our people
and I asked for God's help to make good that vow. Although that vow
was made in my salad days, when I was green in judgement,
I do not regret nor retract one word of it."*

Queen Elizabeth, Silver Jubilee speech, 7th June 1977

RIGHT: The Queen greets crowds during the Scottish leg of the Jubilee tour, 24th May 1977.

The Queen's Silver Jubilee year was commemorated with thousands of street parties up and down the country as Britain came together to celebrate.

The actual anniversary of her accession to the throne, on 6th February 1977, was marked by a low-key church service at St George's Chapel, Windsor. But the main "Jubilee Day" celebrations, in June that year, saw Britain come to a standstill to cheer its much-loved queen.

Preparations for the parties started as early as March, as families across the land festooned their homes and streets with bunting and joined with their neighbours to eat, drink and party.

In an Address to Parliament on 4th May the Queen told the House of Commons "a Jubilee is a time to look forward" and said: "May it also be a time in which we can all draw closer together." She added: "These 25 years have seen much change for Britain. By virtue of tolerance and understanding, the Empire has evolved into a Commonwealth of 36 Independent Nations spanning five continents. No longer an Imperial Power, we have been coming to terms with what this means for ourselves and our relations with the rest of the world."

On 6th June the Queen lit a bonfire beacon at Windsor Castle, which started a chain of beacons across the country. The following day, in glorious sunshine, more than 1 million people lined the streets of London, and another 500 million watched on TV, as the Royal Family made their way to a service of thanksgiving at St Paul's Cathedral. Crowds cheered as the family passed in the Golden State Coach to join world leaders, including Prime Minister James Callaghan and US President Jimmy Carter, for the

BELOW: Crowds dance in the street during a Silver Jubilee street party in Radcot and Methley streets, south London, 7th June 1977.

service. Afterwards, the Queen made her Silver Jubilee speech where she thanked the people of Britain and the Commonwealth for the "loyalty and friendship" that had given her "strength and encouragement during these last 25 years". "Liz Rules, OK", was the *Daily Mirror*'s headline the next day, adding: "It was the end of a day to remember … when the Queen won the heart of a nation."

The Jubilee celebrations culminated in a procession down the River Thames from Greenwich to Lambeth on 9th June, re-enacting the elaborate barge trips of Queen Elizabeth I and ending in a spectacular fireworks display.

That year Elizabeth and Philip also undertook an epic tour round the UK and Commonwealth, travelling 56,000 miles in 12 months. Throughout February and March they visited Western Samoa, Australia, New Zealand, Tonga,

Fiji, Tasmania, Papua New Guinea, Bombay and Oman, and from May until August the couple toured the whole of the UK and Northern Ireland, visiting 36 counties in just three months in a feat unmatched by any other sovereign. The year ended with visits to Canada and the Caribbean in October, before the Queen headed back home to spend Christmas with her family, including her new baby grandson. Queen Elizabeth was delighted to become a grandmother for the first time when Princess Anne gave birth to Peter Phillips on 15th November.

In her Christmas speech she summed up the happy events of 1977 by telling the country: "The street parties and village fêtes, the presents, the flowers from the children, the mile upon mile of decorated streets and houses; these things suggest that the real value and pleasure of the celebration was that we all shared in it together."

ABOVE: The Queen, Prince Philip, Prince Charles and Prince Andrew at the Windsor Castle bonfire celebrations, where the Queen lit the first of many Silver Jubilee beacons round the country, 6th June 1977.

LEFT: **Crowds flood the streets outside Buckingham Palace to see the Queen on the balcony during the Silver Jubilee, 7th June 1977.**

ABOVE: The Queen and Prince Philip arrive at St Paul's Cathedral for the Silver Jubilee thanksgiving service, 7th June 1977.

LEFT: Silver Jubilee street party in Kirkley Drive, Ashington, Northumberland, 7th June 1977.

RIGHT: The Queen and the Lord Mayor of London walk to the Guildhall for lunch after the Silver Jubilee thanksgiving service at St Paul's Cathedral, 7th June 1977.

ABOVE: **The Queen and Prince Philip return from St Paul's Cathedral after a Silver Jubilee service of thanksgiving, 7th June 1977.**

ABOVE: **The Queen and Prince Philip are presented with a whale's tooth in Fiji during the Silver Jubilee tour, 16th February 1977.**

ABOVE: **Wearing a Maori ceremonial cloak, the Queen chats with tribesmen at the rugby ground in Gisborne, New Zealand, during the Silver Jubilee tour, February 1977.**

BELOW: **The Queen watches an exhibition of local spinning in Christchurch, New Zealand, during the Silver Jubilee tour, February 1977.**

LEFT: The Queen and Prince Philip wave goodbye from the royal train at Euston station on 16th May 1977 as they begin the first leg of their UK Silver Jubilee tour. The tour began in Glasgow on 17th May and finished in Derry, Northern Ireland, on 11th August.

ABOVE: **The Queen looks at home on Wimbledon's Centre Court after presenting Britain's Virginia Wade with her trophy for winning Wimbledon, 4th July 1977. Wade beat Holland's Betty Stöve in the final.**

LEFT: **Ballerina Margot Fonteyn curtseys to the Queen as dance partner Rudolf Nureyev looks on after the Queen's Silver Jubilee Gala at the Royal Opera House in Covent Garden, 30th May 1977.**

ABOVE: The Queen leaving Grampian Police Force Headquarters after officially opening the building on the Scottish leg of her Silver Jubilee tour, 23rd May 1977.

LEFT: The Queen meets schoolchildren in Cramlington High School, Northumberland, during the northeast leg of the Silver Jubilee tour, July 1977.

ABOVE: **The Queen in the crowd after opening Eldon shopping centre in Newcastle during the Silver Jubilee tour, 15th July 1977.**

LEFT: **The Queen on a walkabout in Durham during the Silver Jubilee tour, 14th July 1977.**

ABOVE: **Princess Anne with her son, Peter Phillips, at his baptism at Buckingham Palace, 22nd December 1977. Peter was born at St Mary's Hospital in Paddington, and the Queen was one of the first visitors. Princess Anne and her husband Captain Mark Phillips chose not to give him a title, a decision they also made for their daughter Zara, who was born four years later.**

RIGHT: **The Queen, Prince Philip, their four children and grandson Peter Phillips at Balmoral, 1st November 1979.**

CHAPTER SIX

CHANGING TIMES
1978 – 1991

"The context of the lives of the next generation is being set, here and now…
by the example of our attitudes and behaviour to one another…"

Queen Elizabeth, Christmas broadcast, 1978

RIGHT: The Queen and the Queen Mother during the state visit of the Queen of the Netherlands, November 1982.

WOMEN OF DESTINY

Britain elected its first female prime minister in May 1979, and for the first time in the country's history two women were at its helm.

Margaret Thatcher proved to be a controversial leader, but voters were full of hope when she stood on the steps of 10 Downing Street on 4th May and, quoting from St Francis of Assisi, said: "Where there is discord, may we bring harmony."

Like every prime minister, Thatcher held weekly meetings with the Queen throughout her leadership, which lasted for more than 11 years.

Just a few months after she was elected, in August 1979, the Royal Family was plunged into despair when the Queen's cousin was killed by an IRA bomb on his fishing boat in Ireland. Lord Mountbatten, 79, had been a close confidant to both Prince Philip and Prince Charles, and his sudden death brought the conflict in Northern Ireland right to the heart of the Royal Family.

That year also brought another unwelcome surprise for the Queen when her art adviser, Sir Anthony Blunt, was publicly unmasked as a Soviet spy and immediately stripped of his knighthood.

But the following decade, the 1980s, kicked off with celebration for the Queen.

The Queen Mother marked her 80th birthday with a thanksgiving service in July 1980, and her popularity with the people was clear from the thousands that lined the streets, singing and cheering. And, shortly after, another woman, this time very young, was to generate never-before-seen levels of excitement and interest in the Royal Family.

Prince Charles announced his engagement to 19-year-old Lady Diana Spencer on 24th February 1981. By this time the country longed to see the 32-year-old heir to the throne settle down, and Diana was considered a perfect match for him: a young, beautiful, virgin bride from an aristocratic family. She was nicknamed "Shy Di", and the public instantly fell in love with her warm, girlish demeanour. However, the couple had been together for less than a year when they announced they would marry, and there were ominous signs from the start. For example, in their engagement interview, when asked if they were in love, Charles now notoriously replied: "Whatever 'in love' means."

Nevertheless, the wedding five months later at St Paul's Cathedral was a spectacular success, and a day that catapulted the royals onto the world stage like never before. The image of the bride in her Emanuel dress with its 25-foot train saw the young girl from Norfolk achieve iconic status and an unprecedented level of adulation.

A nervous Diana mixed up her husband's name in her vows, but recovered to give the Queen a beautiful curtsey after the couple said "I do", and the newlyweds emerged from the Cathedral to the shrieks of the thousands who had lined the streets, while a record 750 million watched from their homes.

After processing through London, Charles and Diana delighted crowds by being the first royal couple to kiss on the Buckingham Palace balcony. "My Princess", said the *Daily Mirror* the next day, "The joy of a couple in love".

Less than a year later the Queen's most famous grandchild was born, when Diana gave birth to an heir, William, in June 1982, followed by a "spare", brother Harry, two years later.

By February 1982 the Queen had been on the throne for 30 years. Now well into her 50s, she had become one of the country's greatest assets, a long-standing symbol of its traditions and values. But the nation was reminded she was also a mother when she waved off her son Prince Andrew to fight in the Falklands War in 1982.

When Argentina invaded the Falkland Islands on 2nd April Andrew's ship the HMS *Invincible* was sent to defend the British territory. The Queen had insisted he be allowed to remain with his crew, but she was anxious until the day he safely returned to Portsmouth in September, victorious, for a hero's welcome.

A bizarre incident had also catapulted the Queen into the spotlight earlier that year when she woke up to find an intruder at the end of her bed. Michael Fagan scaled the walls of Buckingham Palace and spent 10 minutes talking to Elizabeth as she lay in her nightgown before help came. "Break in at the Palace", was the *Daily Mirror*'s headline, "Security checks after royal guards seize an intruder." As trespassing was then a civil offence Fagan was never charged, but the incident sparked calls for tougher palace security.

But no amount of security fears would ever stop the Queen from carrying out her royal duties, and she travelled extensively during the early 1980s, visiting Canada several times, and also America, Australia, Kenya, Jamaica, Papua New Guinea, Fiji and many more countries.

Her state visit to India in November 1983 brought about a historic meeting with Mother Teresa. "Women of destiny", said the *Daily Mirror* as the two great women spoke.

The following year the Queen led the D-Day 40th anniversary celebrations in Normandy, announcing in her Christmas broadcast that year: "For me, perhaps the most lasting impression was one of thankfulness that the forty intervening years have been ones of comparative peace."

ABOVE: **The Queen and her mother at the thanksgiving service at St Paul's Cathedral for the Queen Mother's 80th birthday, 15th July 1980.**

ABOVE: **The Queen and her racing manager, Lord Porchester, watch the finish of the 1978 Derby, 8ᵗʰ June 1978.**

ABOVE: **The Queen taking a picture at the Royal Windsor Horse Trials, 17th May 1981.**

LEFT: **The Queen and Prince Philip visit Pompeii on a trip to Italy, 19th October 1980.**

ROYAL WEDDING

ABOVE: **Crowds line the streets of London for the wedding of Prince Charles to Lady Diana Spencer, 29th July 1981.**

ABOVE: Lady Diana Spencer arrives at St Paul's Cathedral on her wedding day to Prince Charles, 29th July 1981.

LEFT: Prince Charles and new wife Diana, Princess of Wales, leave St Paul's Cathedral after saying their wedding vows, 29th July 1981.

ABOVE: Prince Charles and Diana ride to Buckingham Palace for their wedding reception after saying their vows at St Paul's Cathedral, 29th July 1981.

ABOVE: The Royal Family with Prince Charles and Princess Diana on the Buckingham Palace balcony on their wedding day, 29th July 1981. Two months before the wedding Princess Anne had given birth to her second child, Zara Phillips, born on 15th May 1981.

LEFT: Prince Charles and Diana drive to Waterloo to travel to their honeymoon after their wedding day celebrations, 29th July 1981.

ABOVE: **Prince Charles and Princess Diana on their honeymoon on the Royal Yacht Britannia, 1st August 1981.**

LEFT: **The Queen with Prince Charles and a bored-looking Princess Diana at the Braemar Games, 5th September 1981, two months after the couple were married. The Highland Games are one of the staple events in the royal calendar.**

BELOW: **The Queen, Queen Mother and Princess Diana in the royal box at Ascot; date unknown.**

LEFT: The Queen plants a tree after she opens Kielder Reservoir in Northumberland, May 1982.

RIGHT: The Queen with Pope John Paul II on his historic visit to Britain, the first by a pope for 450 years, 31st May 1982.

ABOVE: **Princess Diana with Prince William leaving hospital accompanied by Prince Charles in June 1982.**

RIGHT: **Princess Diana and Prince Charles with their newborn son, Prince William, pose for an official photograph with the Queen, Prince Philip and the Queen Mother, June 1982.**

LEFT: **The Queen riding at Windsor with US President Ronald Regan, during the President's state visit to Britain, 9th June 1982.**

BELOW: **The Queen roars with laughter as she talks to shot-put champion Geoff Capes at the Braemar Games, 4th September 1982.**

ABOVE: **Prince Andrew cheers as he returns from service in the Falklands as a Sea King helicopter co-pilot, 17ᵗʰ September 1982.**

ABOVE: The Queen, Prince Philip and Prince Andrew disembark HMS *Invincible* as Andrew safely returns from service in the Falklands War, 17th September 1982.

ABOVE: The Queen and President Regan toast each other at the De Young Museum in San Francisco during a royal tour of America's West Coast, March 1983.

RIGHT: The Queen salutes during Trooping the Colour, 16th June 1984. She is on her favourite horse, Burmese, a black mare who was given to her by the Canadian Mounted Police in 1969 when she was seven. The Queen rode her at Trooping the Colour every year from then until the mare was retired in 1986. Her most dramatic appearance was in 1981 when a 17-year-old fired six blank shots at the Queen. Burmese was startled but the Queen brought her under control. The teenage attacker, Marcus Simon Serjeant, was later jailed for five years under the 1842 Treason Act. Burmese died four years after her retirement in 1990.

OPPOSITE: The Queen and Prince Philip with Indian Prime Minister Indira Gandhi on a royal visit to India, November 1983. Indira was assassinated a year later on 15th October 1984.

ABOVE: **Prince Charles and Princess Diana with their two sons, Prince William, born on 21st June 1982, and Prince Harry, born on 15th September 1984.**

LEFT: The Queen gets a kiss from Prince Charles after she presents him with a trophy for his winning polo team, 30th July 1985.

RIGHT: The Queen and Prime Minister Margaret Thatcher celebrate the 250th anniversary of 10 Downing Street, 4th December 1985.

ROCKY RELATIONSHIPS

"There are many serious and threatening problems in this country and in the world but they will never be solved until there is peace in our homes and love in our hearts."

Queen Elizabeth, Christmas broadcast, December 1986

ABOVE: **The Queen at the Tall Ships Race in Newcastle, 19th July 1986.**

In 1986 the Queen was delighted when Prince Andrew announced his engagement to fun-loving redhead Sarah Ferguson. Often rumoured to be her favourite son, it looked like playboy prince Andrew had found his perfect match in feisty Sarah, who became the Duchess of York after the wedding but was quickly nicknamed Fergie.

But, as Andrew's married life began, rumours were already rife that Charles and Diana were on the brink of separation. As early as the mid 1980s cracks began to appear in their relationship, and there was speculation both were having affairs – Charles with his ex Camilla Parker Bowles and Diana with army officer James Hewitt.

By this time the public's deferential attitude to the monarchy was starting to be replaced by a more scrutinizing one, and reporting of the Royal Family's dysfunctional relationships was rife. And while aides constantly tried to dampen any suggestions of rifts, in October 1989 they were forced to announce that Princess Anne was separating from Captain Mark Phillips. After 16 years together and two children the marriage was over, and it soon emerged that the princess was seeing another man, the Queen's equerry, Captain Timothy Laurence.

By 1990 Andrew and Sarah's short marriage was also breaking down, and the Queen's job as head of the family was more challenging than ever. But, through all the furore, she ploughed on with her duties, again and again proving herself to be a stable figure in an ever changing landscape.

On 16th May 1991, in the wake of victory in the Gulf War, she became the first British head of state to address a joint meeting of Congress on a state visit to the US. She told them: "The future is, as ever, obscure. The only certainty is that it will present the world with new and daunting problems."

ABOVE: **Prince Andrew and bride Sarah Ferguson, the new Duke and Duchess of York, walk through the arch at Westminster Abbey on their wedding day, 23rd July 1986.**

LEFT: **The Royal Family on the balcony of Buckingham Palace after the wedding of Prince Andrew and Sarah Ferguson, 23rd July 1986.**

LEFT: The Queen and Prince Philip, with Chinese President Li Xiannian, reviewing the guard of honour at their official welcoming ceremony on a royal visit to China, 13th October 1986. This was the trip where Philip made one of his most notorious gaffes, telling a group of British exchange students living in Xian: "If you stay here much longer you'll all be slitty-eyed."

BELOW: The Queen prepares to eat sea slugs at a banquet in Beijing, 14th October 1986.

LEFT: The Queen on her 60th birthday, being given flowers by children, 21st April 1986.

BELOW: Members of the Royal Family in costume taking part in a one-off charity production of TV's *It's A Knockout*, filmed at Alton Towers, 19th June 1987. The production was staged by 23-year-old Prince Edward who persuaded the Duke and Duchess of York and Princess Anne to take part. The incident is often looked back on as an embarrassment to the royals.

ABOVE: **The Royal Family outside the Church of St Mary Magdalene in Sandringham after Princess Eugenie's christening, the second daughter of Andrew and Sarah on 23rd December 1990. She was born on 23rd March 1990, two years after her older sister Beatrice, who was born on 8th August 1988. Eugenie was the first royal baby to have a public christening.**

LEFT: **The Queen with her grandchildren Peter and Zara Phillips and Princes William and Harry, 11th January 1988.**

RIGHT: **The Queen with three-year-old Princess Beatrice, 12th May 1991.**

CHAPTER SEVEN

ANNUS HORRIBILIS
1992

*"1992 is not a year I shall look back on with undiluted pleasure.
In the words of one of my more sympathetic correspondents, it has turned out
to be an 'Annus Horribilis'."*

Queen Elizabeth, Annus Horribilis speech marking the 40th anniversary of her accession, 24th November 1992

RIGHT: The Queen gives her Annus Horribilis speech, 24th November 1992.

Although every year of the Queen's reign had its ups and downs, in 1992 disaster after disaster seemed to hit the royals.

Speculation that Andrew and Fergie's marriage was rocky was confirmed in March when, exactly six years after their engagement, Buckingham Palace issued a statement announcing their separation. In a rare and unprecedented move the statement detailed the Queen's unhappiness at the matter, saying she found it "undesirable" during the country's general election campaign. The statement said: "Last week lawyers acting for the Duchess of York initiated discussions about a formal separation for the Duke and Duchess."

Just one month later, a few days after the Conservatives won the general election With John Major as their prime minister, Princess Anne divorced Mark Phillips. By now they had been separated for three years and, although inevitable, the day the first of her children became officially divorced was not a moment the Queen relished.

Furthermore, Charles and Diana, the couple that had barely been out of the spotlight since their wedding, saw interest in their marriage hit fever pitch in June 1992 when Diana's unofficial biography was published. *Diana: Her True Story* by Andrew Morton lifted the lid on Diana's unhappiness, detailing the rejection she felt by Charles and the Royal Family, her battles with bulimia and alleging that she had tried to kill herself as many as five times during the 1980s.

The book's unflattering portrayal of the Queen as cold and inhuman must have hurt her deeply.

Coverage of the book went into overdrive and the *Daily Mirror* published a Royal Crisis Special where it asked: "Is this woman [Diana] unhappy enough to try and take her own life?" One week later its front page pictured her and Charles

looking miserable at the annual Garter Ceremony with the headline: "Unhappy and glorious. Together but so far apart." Their separation was announced on 9th December 1992.

If her worries over Charles and Diana weren't enough, Andrew and Sarah's marriage continued to cause problems for the Queen even after their separation. In August, when

RIGHT: **Windsor Castle on fire, 20th November 1992.**

184

Fergie was staying with the royals at Balmoral, the *Daily Mirror* published pictures of her cavorting topless with her financial adviser John Bryan. The now infamous "toe sucking" photographs heaped yet more embarrassment on the family.

And in November things literally went up in smoke when the Queen's beloved Windsor Castle went on fire after a spotlight ignited a curtain.

Three days after Elizabeth toured the castle ruins she made one of her most famous speeches to mark the 40th anniversary of her accession. Describing the year as an "Annus Horribilis" she concluded: "Distance is well known to lend enchantment even to less attractive views."

LEFT: **The Royal Family on the Queen Mother's 92nd birthday, 4th August 1992.**

BELOW: **The Queen, Queen Mother, Prince Charles and Princess Diana at Trooping the Colour on 13th June 1992, just a few days after Andrew Morton's biography *Diana: Her True Story* was published.**

ABOVE: **Princess Diana, Princess Anne and the Queen Mother on Remembrance Sunday, 8th November 1992. Diana's separation from Charles was announced one month later.**

ABOVE: **The Queen tours the site of fire-ravaged Windsor Castle, 20ᵗʰ November 1992.**

CHAPTER EIGHT

MOVING FORWARD
1993 – 2001

"If we can look on the bright side, so much the better, but that does not mean we should shield ourselves from the truth, even if it is unwelcome."

Queen Elizabeth, Christmas broadcast, 1993

RIGHT: The Queen and Princess Diana at the wedding of the Queen's nephew Lord Linley to Serena Stanhope, 8th October 1993.

KEEPING GOING

The 1990s had got off to a rocky start for the Royal Family, but the Queen was determined to pick up the pieces and carry on.

In the summer of 1993 Buckingham Palace was open to visitors for the first time to help raise the £40 million needed to repair Windsor Castle, after there was widespread opposition to the idea of using taxpayers' money. The Queen was not at home during the opening but it proved to be a huge success and the tradition has continued ever since.

The Nineties was a decade when communication and technology rapidly expanded and the internet and mobile phones became a staple part of every home and workplace. The world grew smaller and the Queen paid state visits to many places including Hungary in 1993, Russia in 1994, and Poland and the Czech Republic in 1996.

History was also made with a visit to post-apartheid South Africa in 1995 just after Nelson Mandela won the 1994 election to become the country's first black president. In a speech the Queen said: "Forty-eight years ago I watched my father opening Parliament here … Of course, I come here in very different circumstances but, ever since that visit, I have felt that my memories of South Africa are part of me, and I have wanted to return to this magnificent country."

But problems that had been simmering at home came back with a vengeance in 1995 when Princess Diana gave an interview on TV's *Panorama*. She described her introduction to royal life as "isolating", admitted to self-harming, post-natal depression and bulimia, and told interviewer Martin Bashir she knew Charles was in love with Camilla Parker Bowles, adding "there were three of us in this marriage".

The damning interview was the final straw for the Queen. Worried about the effect their relationship problems were having on the monarchy, she wrote to the couple asking them to divorce, and their marriage officially ended in August 1996.

A year later the country's relationship with its government also had an overhaul when Labour's Tony Blair was elected prime minister after 18 years of Conservative rule. The landslide victory marked a fresh chapter in Britain's politics, but the Queen continued to play a key role, making her usual speech at the official opening of Parliament that month.

With a new government bringing the country a feeling of optimism, and with her children's marriage problems seemingly nipped in the bud, it looked like the struggles of the past decade had turned a corner. But no one was prepared for what happened next.

RIGHT: The Queen has tears in her eyes as, on 17ᵗʰ March 1996, she views the site of the Dunblane Massacre, where a gunman let loose in a primary school killing 16 pupils and their teacher on 13ᵗʰ March 1996.

ABOVE: **The Queen views the workings of the Alcan Aluminium Smelting Works, Lynemouth, 26th June 1993.**

ABOVE: **President of the Russian Federation, Boris Yeltsin, appears to touch the Queen's bottom during her historic visit to the Kremlin in Moscow, 18th October 1994.**

RIGHT: **The Queen looks solemn as she watches the 50th anniversary Remembrance Day parade in London, 12th November 1995.**

ABOVE: The Queen with South African President Nelson Mandela on the first day of his state visit to the UK on 9th July 1996. In April 1995 she had visited post-apartheid South Africa, the first time she had been there since 1947.

ABOVE: **New Prime Minister Tony Blair outside Downing Street after visiting the Queen on 2nd May 1997, following his landslide victory in the 1997 general election. In his memoirs *A Journey*, published in 2010, he later wrote that she told him: "You are my 10th Prime Minister. The first was Winston. That was before you were born."**

DEVASTATION

"What I say to you now, as your queen and as a grandmother, I say from my heart. First, I want to pay tribute to Diana myself."

Queen Elizabeth on the eve of Princess Diana's funeral, 5th September 1997

RIGHT: The Queen and Prince Philip arrive at Buckingham Palace. Stopping the car they go walkabout and look at the flowers as well as talking to members of the public.

During the middle of the night on 31st August 1997 Princess Diana was killed in a car crash in the Pont de l'Alma tunnel in Paris.

Her sudden death rocked Britain to its core. The country could not believe the woman who had delighted and captivated them for almost 20 years, the "People's Princess", was no more. "Home to a nation mourning", the *Daily Mirror* said as her coffin was brought back to Britain.

The Royal Family were at Balmoral when the news broke, and were faced with the grief of two teenage boys who had lost their mother.

But the Queen's failure to make an announcement or be seen publicly soon sparked a backlash. "Your people are suffering. Speak to us Ma'am", was the *Daily Mirror*'s headline on 4th September. In response the Queen's press secretary issued a statement saying: "The Royal Family have been hurt by suggestions that they are indifferent to the country's sorrow at the tragic death of the Princess of Wales." The following day the Queen and Prince Philip returned to London, stopping to look at the blanket of flowers and cards that festooned the gates of Buckingham Palace.

More than a million people lined the route from Kensington Palace to Westminster Abbey on 6th September for Diana's funeral. The crowd wept as William, 15, and Harry, 12, walked behind their mother's coffin on a day that marked an outpouring of grief never before seen in the UK.

RIGHT: Princess Diana's coffin is carried through the streets of London on her funeral, 6th September 1997.

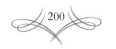

LEFT: **The Queen and Queen Mother arrive at Westminster Abbey for Princess Diana's funeral, 6ᵗʰ September 1997.**

RIGHT: **Princes William and Harry flanked by Prince Charles and Earl Spencer walking behind their mother's coffin as crowds line the streets in mourning, 6ᵗʰ September 1997.**

PICKING UP THE PIECES

"For us, a Royal Family, however, the message is often harder to read, obscured as it can be by deference, rhetoric or the conflicting currents of public opinion.
But read it we must.
I have done my best, with Prince Philip's constant love and help, to interpret it correctly through the years of our marriage and of my reign as your queen."

Queen Elizabeth, golden wedding anniversary speech,
20th November 1997

RIGHT: The Queen opens the new Children's Hospital in Birmingham, now called the Diana Princess of Wales Children's Hospital, October 1998.

LEFT: **The Queen and Prince Philip at a museum opening, 30th November 1998.**

BELOW: **The Queen on a walkabout in Dundee, 30th June 1998.**

Three months after Diana's death the Queen and Prince Philip marked their golden wedding anniversary. With the royals and the country still mourning, the celebrations were low-key. But the Queen made a heartfelt speech at London's Guildhall where she thanked her husband for being her "strength and stay" throughout the years.

She also chose the moment to touch on the challenges faced by a hereditary monarchy in a modern democracy, and reflected on the huge changes Britain had seen since she and Philip married in post-war Britain. "What a remarkable fifty years they have been: For the world, for the Commonwealth and for Britain," she said. "Think what we would have missed if we had never heard the Beatles or seen Margot Fonteyn dance: never have watched television, used a mobile telephone or surfed the Net."

Now in that she was in her 70s, the Queen's grandchildren were already adults, with Prince Charles celebrating his 50th birthday in November 1998.

The following summer her youngest son, Edward, married career woman Sophie Rhys-Jones at St George's Chapel, Windsor. The Queen made them the Earl and Countess of Wessex on their wedding day, and Edward is the only one of her children to remain happily married. The wedding was relatively low-key by royal standards, but in August 2000 thousands took to the streets to celebrate the Queen Mother's 100th birthday.

Considered by many to be a national treasure, the Queen Mother inspired genuine affection from the public, who cheered as she waved from the balcony of Buckingham Palace. She is the only member of the Royal Family to reach the age of 100.

The country was now in a new millennium, but with exciting new developments there also came new challenges and threats.

The Western world was rocked to its core when al-Qaeda terrorists launched a large-scale attack on America, crashing two planes into the Twin Towers of the World Trade Center and killing almost 3,000 people. The Queen made the attack the focus of her Christmas broadcast that year, telling Britain: "During the following days we struggled to find ways of expressing our horror at what had happened …

"I hope that in the months to come we shall all be able to find ways of strengthening our own communities as a sure support and comfort to us all – whatever may lie ahead."

LEFT: **Prince Edward and bride Sophie Rhys-Jones, the new Earl and Countess of Wessex, with the Queen after their wedding at St George's Chapel, Windsor Castle, 19th June 1999.**

BELOW: **The Queen joins hands with Prime Minister Tony Blair, Prince Philip and Cherie Blair to sing 'Auld Lang Syne' bringing in the New Year at the Millennium Dome, 1st January 2000.**

LEFT: The Queen Mother is greeted by the Lord Mayor of London at the St Paul's Cathedral thanksgiving service celebrating her 100th birthday. Prince Charles, William and Harry look on, 11th July 2000.

BELOW: Princess Margaret, the Queen Mother and the Queen acknowledge the crowds from Buckingham Palace on the Queen Mother's 100th birthday, 4th August 2000.

LEFT: The Royal Family watch horse racing through binoculars, 20th September 2000.

BELOW: The Queen with President Clinton, his wife Hilary and his daughter Chelsea on their last presidential visit to the UK, 14th December 2000.

LEFT: **The Queen looks solemn as she attends a memorial service at St Paul's Cathedral for the victims of the September 11 attacks, 14th September 2001.**

BELOW: **The Queen meets pop singer Jennifer Lopez after the Royal Variety Show, 26th November 2001.**

CHAPTER NINE

GOLDEN JUBILEE
2002

"For if a Jubilee becomes a moment to define an age, then for me we must speak of change – its breadth and accelerating pace over these years."

Queen Elizabeth, Golden Jubilee address to Parliament, 30th April 2002

RIGHT: **The Queen and Prince Philip return along the Mall to Buckingham Palace after the Jubilee parade, 4th June 2002.**

Although her Golden Jubilee was a time of celebration, the year began with tragedy for the Queen.

After battling a series of health problems and suffering strokes that left her paralysed and damaged her sight, Princess Margaret died on 9th February 2002, aged 71. She was remembered by those close to her for her "vivaciousness" and "vitality", and, despite her turbulent relationships, friends said she had a "happy" life and revealed that she adored her older sister. Friend Lord St John of Fawsley said: "I never in all my life heard Princess Margaret say a harsh or critical word about the Queen. She was totally devoted to her."

And the Queen had even more sadness to bear when, just six weeks later, her beloved mother died. Aged 101, the Queen Mother had led a long and fulfilling life, and she passed away peacefully at the Royal Lodge, Windsor, on 30th March with the Queen by her side.

As one of the most loved members of the Royal Family, her death sparked a huge outpouring of grief from the British public. Thousands of bouquets were strewn across the railings of Clarence House and Buckingham Palace as Prime Minister Tony Blair led the tributes, describing how her "zest for life made her loved and admired by people of all ages and backgrounds, revered within our borders and beyond".

Losing two of the people closest to her in the world during what should have been one of her most joyful years was devastating for the Queen. But, as always, she put her duty to her country before her personal troubles, and channelled her energies into making her Golden Jubilee a success.

She spent the 50th anniversary of her accession to the throne – 6th February – meeting cancer patients while opening

the Macmillan Centre at the Queen Elizabeth Hospital in Norfolk. On the same day she issued a message to the nation saying: "I believe that, young or old, we have as much to look forward to with confidence and hope as we have to look back on with pride." The message was posted on the new British monarchy website, a sign of the changing times that the crown was determined to embrace.

In her Golden Jubilee address to Parliament in April the

ABOVE: The Royal Family on the 101st birthday of the Queen Mother, 4th August 2001. This was Princess Margaret's second-last appearance in public before her death on 9th February 2002 and there was grave concern for her health after she was pictured at the celebrations, with reports describing her as "frail" and "bloated".

Queen also paid heed to the "transformation" of Britain since she came to the throne. She said: "Since 1952 I have witnessed the transformation of the international landscape through which this country must chart its course …

"This has been matched by no less rapid developments at home, in the devolved shape of our nation, in the structure of society, in technology and communications, in our work and in the way we live."

But, somehow, through all the changes, the Queen had managed to remain at the heart of Britain, her presence a welcome constant in a rapidly altering world.

In the run-up to the Golden Jubilee there were critics who speculated the event wouldn't be a success, and that people were no longer enthused by the monarchy. But the main celebrations from 1st to 4th June proved them all wrong. More than 2 million people applied for tickets for the Saturday night Prom in the Palace, and 12,500 were chosen to attend what was the largest event ever held on royal property.

Two days later the palace was home to another concert, this time a pop extravaganza, where performers included Paul McCartney, Eric Clapton, Cliff Richard and Queen guitarist Brian May. The evening culminated in a spectacular fireworks display as the Queen lit a beacon in the Mall, the last of more than 2,000 beacons round the world. About 12,000 people were invited to the concert, more than a million flooded the Mall, and a further 2 million watched

from their homes. "The Golden Smile" was the *Daily Mirror*'s headline the next day.

The final day of the Jubilee weekend saw the Queen and Prince Philip parade through London in the Golden State Coach to attend a national service of thanksgiving at St Paul's Cathedral, before watching a spectacular parade and flypast over Buckingham Palace. That day the Queen said: "Gratitude, respect and pride, these words sum up how I feel about the people of this country and the Commonwealth – and what this Golden Jubilee means to me."

That year, as with her Silver Jubilee, the Queen and Philip toured Britain and the world, travelling more than 40,000 miles by air to countries such as Jamaica, New Zealand, Australia and Canada, and visiting 70 UK cities and towns.

ABOVE: **The Queen Mother clutches flowers from the public on her 101st birthday, 4th August 2001. Just three days earlier she had been taken to hospital and had to have a blood transfusion after being diagnosed with anaemia. But, determined not to disappoint well-wishers, she waved to crowds outside Clarence House for 40 minutes as they sang 'Happy Birthday'.**

LEFT: The Queen on the 50th anniversary of her succession to the throne, opening the cancer unit of the Queen Elizabeth Hospital, King's Lynn, 6th February 2002.

BELOW: The Queen, dressed in black, attends an engagement re-opening the Salvation Army's William Booth House in London's East End on 12th February 2002, three days after her sister's death.

RIGHT: The Royal Family make their way to the funeral of Princess Margaret at St George's Chapel, Windsor, 15th February 2002. The funeral, held on the 50th anniversary of her father King George VI's funeral, was a private event for family and friends.

LEFT: The Queen Mother's coffin parades towards Westminster Abbey, followed by nine members of the Royal Family, for her state funeral. After her death on 30th March she was taken to lie in state in Westminster Hall as her beloved husband King George VI had been more than 50 years before. In excess of 200,000 people came to pay their respects at her coffin and about 1 million lined the route to the service at Westminster Abbey on 9th April 2002. There was a two-minute silence when her coffin arrived at 11.30am. She was laid to rest alongside her husband in St George's Chapel, Windsor. The ashes of Princess Margaret were interred at the same time.

BELOW: Prince Andrew, Prince Charles, the Duke of Edinburgh and Princess Anne walk behind the Queen Mother's coffin.

LEFT: Madame Tussauds celebrates the Golden Jubilee by removing the ropes around the Queen's waxwork, 7th May 2002.

BELOW: The Queen on the first day of her Golden Jubilee tour at Falmouth railway station in Cornwall, 1st May 2002.

ABOVE: **The Queen visits Durham Gala theatre during her Golden Jubilee tour.**

LEFT: Crowds in the Mall for the Queen's Golden Jubilee, 4th June 2002.

BELOW: The Queen leaves Buckingham Palace in the Golden State Coach to make her way to St Paul's Cathedral for a service of thanksgiving, 4th June 2002. This was followed by lunch at the Guildhall, where she made a speech.

RIGHT: Crowds cheer the Queen as she travels in the Golden State Coach on the final day of the Golden Jubilee celebrations, 4th June 2002.

LEFT: Fireworks over Buckingham Palace after the pop concert, 3rd June 2002.

BELOW: The Queen visits Slough during her Golden Jubilee celebrations, 3rd June 2002.

CHAPTER TEN

A MODERN QUEEN
2003 – 2012

"Our modern world places such heavy demands on our time and attention that the need to remember our responsibilities to others is greater than ever."

Queen Elizabeth, Christmas broadcast, 2002

RIGHT: The Queen smiles as she attends a garden party at Loughry College, Cookstown during the Golden Jubilee visit to Northern Ireland, 14th May 2002.

A NEW AGE

The success of the Golden Jubilee celebrations had cemented the Queen's place at the heart of Britain as it forged into the 21st century.

One of only a handful of monarchs ever to reign for more than 50 years, Elizabeth could now be confident that her place in history as a long-standing and much-loved queen was secured. Nevertheless, she showed no signs of slowing down. Despite being well into her 70s, an age when most people are enjoying their retirement, the Queen continued to attend hundreds of royal engagements every year.

In 2003 she visited Nigeria for the 18th Commonwealth Heads of Government Meeting, and in 2004 she travelled to France and Germany, making a poignant speech in Arromanches, Normandy, on the 60th anniversary of the D-Day landings in June. She told the guests: "We are all getting older, and while it is sad that this will be the final parade in Normandy of the Normandy Veterans Association, it must not be forgotten that the members of the Association continue to care for one another; to help each other in need; to support each other in loss and to keep alive the memory of all that you achieved in those crucial days."

Not even the Queen could defy the ageing process. In 2003 she had keyhole surgery to remove torn cartilage on both her knees, the right knee in January and the left in December. And in June 2005 she was forced to miss several engagements after catching a bad cold.

Although she has generally remained in good health throughout her life, as she approached her 80s Britons were reminded their monarch was not immortal and the fate of the Royal Family would eventually lie with her children and grandchildren. And in 2005, her heir Prince Charles married the woman he wants to be by his side when he becomes king.

His wedding to Camilla Parker Bowles on 9th April 2005 came 30 years after their romance first began and, as the Queen put it in her warm speech: "My son is home and dry with the woman he loves."

Their marriage signified a new chapter for the Royal Family as the woman once shunned by the public for "destroying" the fairytale marriage of Charles and Diana was now not just accepted, but embraced by Britain. Almost 70 years after King Edward VIII was forced to abdicate to marry a divorcee, the heir to the throne, a divorced man, was marrying a woman who was also divorced, and the crowds were cheering. Camilla, now the Duchess of Cornwall, wore two cream outfits through the day, and crowds of more than 20,000 gathered outside the Guildhall.

The Queen and Prince Philip did not attend their civil ceremony at Windsor Guildhall, a move courtiers denied was a "snub", but they were among the 800 guests at the blessing afterwards at St George's Chapel in Windsor Castle.

Almost exactly a year later the Queen celebrated her 80th birthday with a walkabout in Windsor town centre, where crowds of 20,000 waved flags and cheered. "The monarch was showered with gifts, cards, flowers and even a birthday cake with 80 lit candles", said the *Daily Mirror*.

And there were more celebrations the following year when she and Philip celebrated their diamond wedding anniversary on 20th November. More than 2,000 guests, including the couple's four children and eight grandchildren, attended a service at Westminster Abbey, where actress

Dame Judi Dench read Andrew Motion's poem "Diamond Wedding". To mark the occasion Buckingham Palace released a photograph of the couple posing exactly as they had on their honeymoon at Broadlands, Hampshire, six decades before.

On 20th March 2008 the Queen achieved another milestone by attending the first ever Maundy service held in Northern Ireland during a historic visit to Armagh.

ABOVE: **The Queen on a walkabout in Windsor on her 80th birthday, 21st April 2006. The band of the Irish Guards played 'Happy Birthday' and thousands cheered as she appeared. She received 20,000 cards and 17,000 birthday emails through her website.**

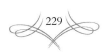

LEFT: **The Queen on a walkabout during a visit to Romford Market, 6ᵗʰ March 2003.**

BELOW: **The Queen and granddaughter Zara Phillips laugh together as they watch the Gold Cup at Cheltenham Racecourse, 13ᵗʰ March 2003.**

ABOVE: **The Queen with President George Bush at a state banquet in Buckingham Palace, 19th November 2003.**

RIGHT: **The Queen with Kate Moss, J K Rowling, Heather Mills and Charlotte Church during a special lunch for women achievers at Buckingham Palace, 11th March 2004.**

LEFT: Prince Charles and new wife Camilla leave Windsor Guildhall after their wedding, 9th April 2005.

BELOW: Prince Charles and new wife Camilla, the Duchess of Cornwall, meet the public after their blessing at St George's Chapel, Windsor, 9th April 2005.

ABOVE: The Queen meets comedian Catherine Tate and singers Charlotte Church and Katherine Jenkins after the Royal Variety Show in Cardiff, 21st November 2005.

RIGHT: The Queen meets Ozzy Osbourne after a pop concert at Buckingham Palace, 17th April 2006.

RIGHT: **The Queen and Philip receive a cake as they tour Guildford after giving out Maundy money at the town cathedral, April 2006.**

LEFT: Prince Harry grins as the Queen inspects his passing out parade at Sandhurst, 12th April 2006.

BELOW: *Sunday Mirror*'s coverage of the wedding of Peter Phillips to Autumn Kelly on 17th May 2008. The wedding caused some controversy for the Royal Family as the couple sold their wedding photographs to *Hello* magazine for £500,000, 18th May 2008.

SECURING THE FUTURE

The two years before the Queen's Diamond Jubilee were among the busiest in history for the Royal Family.

On 16th November 2010 Prince William announced his engagement to long-term girlfriend Kate Middleton. The couple had been dating for eight years after meeting as students at St Andrews University, and news of their wedding was the moment the world had been waiting for. "With this ring … Di thee wed", was the *Daily Mirror*'s headline the following day, highlighting the fact William had chosen to give Kate his late mother's diamond and sapphire engagement ring.

The daughter of a former air hostess and flight dispatcher who became millionaires after going into business selling children's party products, Kate became a global star overnight. A commoner through and through, with a great great grandfather who was a miner, the story of Kate and her prince was hailed as the ultimate modern-day fairytale.

After months of frantic and exciting preparations, the couple were married in Westminster Abbey on 29th April 2011. More than a million people flooded London's Mall to watch them say "I do" and a record 2 billion worldwide watched the ceremony on television. The Queen described the day as "amazing", as the Royal Family enjoyed adulation from round the globe.

Although the wedding showed royal pomp and circumstance at its best, the day was also full of personal, modern touches. "William's eve of ceremony walkabout and the couple's surprise just-married potter down The Mall in a classic Aston Martin sent out a clear message. They are a 21st-century couple who respect tradition – but they will not be slaves to it", said the *Daily Mirror* the next day.

And Kate and William were not the only royals to marry that year. Princess Anne's daughter Zara Phillips said "I do" to England rugby player Mike Tindall in Edinburgh's Canongate Kirk on 30th July 2011. Just like her mother, Zara had grown into a champion horsewoman and no-nonsense royal who won the hearts of the nation by preferring to be recognized for her equestrian skills rather than her bloodline.

Her older brother, Peter Phillips, also gave the Queen something to celebrate in the run-up to her Jubilee when his wife Autumn gave birth to their daughter Savannah on 29th December 2010. Buckingham Palace issued a statement saying that the first-time great-grandparents, the Queen and Prince Philip, were "delighted".

And there was another milestone in May 2011 when the Queen made history as the first British monarch to visit Ireland for 100 years. The last sovereign to make a trip there was her grandfather, George V, in 1911 – 11 years before the country gained independence from Britain.

In a sign that the Queen was leading the way for peace by acknowledging the atrocities of the past, she toured the Croke Park Stadium where 14 people were killed by British forces during a Gaelic football match 91 years earlier. In a

speech she said: "With the benefit of historical hindsight we can all see things which we would wish had been done differently or not at all."

The visit was hailed worldwide as a resounding success, with one commentator summing up the mood by saying if Britain was to choose its own head of state, the Queen would be the best woman for the job.

Just before she visited Ireland, on 12th May 2011, the Queen overtook George III to become Britain's second-longest reigning monarch, outmatched only by Queen Victoria.

The only other British sovereign to have a Diamond Jubilee, Victoria, reigned for 63 years and 216 days. However, as Queen Elizabeth marks the anniversary of her succession to the throne on 6th February 2012, she shows every sign of going on for longer. Buckingham Palace has indicated she has no plans to abdicate, and, as yet, no plans to reduce her workload as she enters the seventh decade of her reign.

Yet, no matter how long the reign of Queen Elizabeth II may be, her place in the history books is already written. It has been written hundreds of times throughout her lifetime and will continue to be written long after she leaves this world. Through her tireless work ethic, her staunch sense of duty and her determination to fulfil her pledge to serve Britain, hers is a story of a truly remarkable woman. In the words of one film critic who reviewed the 2006 Oscar-winning drama *The Queen*, hers is "a story worth telling".

BELOW: **The Queen mingles with guests at a garden party in the grounds of Buckingham Palace, 14th July 2009.**

ABOVE: The Queen chats with the Duke of Kent at Wimbledon's Centre Court, immediately behind the Queen is tennis star Virginia Wade and to her right is Tim Henman, 24th June 2010.

ROYAL WEDDING

RIGHT: **The Queen, Carole Middleton and Camilla, the Duchess of Cornwall outside Westminster Abbey after the wedding of Prince William to Kate Middleton, 29th April 2011. Kate was given away by her father, Michael, her younger sister Pippa was the chief bridesmaid and her brother James did a reading. William's best man was brother Prince Harry.**

ABOVE: **The Queen and Prince Philip arrive at Buckingham Palace after the wedding of Prince William to Kate Middleton, 29th April 2011.**

ABOVE: **The crowds go wild as Prince William and new wife Kate parade through London, 29th April 2011. The couple were made the Duke and Duchess of Cambridge on their wedding day.**

ABOVE: The Royal Family on the balcony of Buckingham Palace after the wedding of Prince William to Kate Middleton, 29th April 2011.

LEFT: Prince William and new wife Kate, kiss on the balcony of Buckingham Palace on their wedding day as four-year-old bridesmaid Grace Van Cutsem covers her ears to drown out the cheering crowds.

RIGHT: The Queen shows US President Barack Obama items on display in Buckingham Palace during his state visit to the UK, 24th May 2011.

LEFT: **The Queen's granddaughter Zara Phillips outside Canongate Kirk, Edinburgh, after her wedding to rugby player Mike Tindall, 30ᵗʰ July 2011.**

RIGHT: **The Queen at the wedding of Zara Phillips to Mike Tindall, 30ᵗʰ July 2011.**

LEFT: The Queen and Irish President Mary McAleese lay a wreath at the War Memorial in Islandbridge, Dublin in a ceremony dedicated to healing divisions between the two countries, 18th May 2011.

"We have much to do together to build a future for all our grandchildren; the kind of future our grandparents could only dream of."

Queen Elizabeth on her visit to Ireland, May 2011

Thanks and acknowledgements

As my first book this publication will always be special to me, but it would not have been possible without the help of many people. I would like to thank Richard Havers and the team at Haynes Publishing for giving me the opportunity to write this book and for their tireless work in helping make it a reality.

It was a privilege to have access to the *Daily Mirror*'s vast picture archives and to discover the incredible images taken 20, 60 and even 90 years ago, and it would have been impossible for me to have done them justice without the expert help of Fergus McKenna and the team at Mirrorpix.

I would also like to thank *Daily Mirror* Editor Richard Wallace, Deputy Editor Peter Willis and Head of Content Chris Bucktin for giving me the opportunity to become Royal Reporter at such an exciting time for the Royal Family, as well as Deputy Managing Editor Aidan McGurran for his support.

Since I started in the role I have got to know many members of the Buckingham Palace and Clarence House press offices and I would like to thank them for being so welcoming and always being ready and willing to assist with any query.

Finally, I would like to thank my nearest and dearest for supporting me unconditionally in everything I choose to do. They are my parents Elizabeth and David, my sisters Caroline and Louise, and my wonderful boyfriend Gary.